LEARNING TO TEACH INCLUSIVELY

Student Teachers' Classroom Inquiries

LEARNING TO TEACH INCLUSIVELY

Student Teachers' Classroom Inquiries

Celia Oyler

and the Preservice Inclusive Study Group

Carine Allaf, Britt Hamre, Scott Howard,
Leslie Gore, Jennifer Lee, Barbara Wang

Teachers College, Columbia University

 LAWRENCE ERLBAUM ASSOCIATES, PUBLISHERS
2006   Mahwah, New Jersey   London

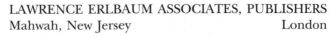

Lawrence Erlbaum Associates, Inc., Publishers
10 Industrial Avenue
Mahwah, New Jersey 07430
www.erlbaum.com

Cover design by Rory Myers

Library of Congress Cataloging-in-Publication Data

Learning to teach inclusively : student teachers' classroom inquiries

ISBN 0-8058-5430-4 (cloth : alk. paper)
ISBN 0-8058-5431-2 (pbk)

Copyright information for this volume can be obtained by contacting
the Library of Congress.

Books published by Lawrence Erlbaum Associates are printed on acid-free paper,
and their bindings are chosen for strength and durability.

Printed in the United States of America
10 9 8 7 6 5 4 3 2 1

Contents

Preface

Almost everyone who has ever been to school has at least one story to tell about feeling left out, criticized, embarrassed, isolated, stupid, or humiliated. In part, this is because schools (in most cases) have acted as sorting machines: designed to reward the students who fit in best and re-shape those whose behaviors challenge the order of things. Yet when I ask the bright-eyed 80 new student teachers each year why they want to be teachers, not one declares, "I want to preserve the natural order of things." Rather, they explain their commitments to: "make a difference in the lives of children," or, "unleash the talent, intelligence, and creativity of individual students," or simply, "to teach a room full of 6 year olds how to read."

Yet the images of learners that many student teachers conjure up do not always include children and youth very different from themselves. Most people who become teachers did not grow up in homeless shelters, or go to bed hungry many nights. Our teachers are mostly drawn from working class and middle class homes, and often seek to teach in the communities from which they hail. And because of the long history in English-speaking countries of "special" institutions and schools for people with disabilities, those home communities and schools did not often include people with disabilities. Just as the Black Power and Civil Rights movements pushed legislation that promised African American children an equal education, so too, has the inclusive education movement created laws that require children with disabilities to be educated alongside their nondisabled peers.

Although inclusive education is still hotly contested in some parts of the English speaking world, many teachers work out the small and large details that allow widely diverse children to learn side-by-side. Certainly, it is not always easy work, particularly in the contexts of high-stakes testing that penalizes schools if students don't score high on such measures. Realizing that the way a student initially qualifies for special education is to have low scores on individual, norm-referenced tests, you can begin to see the disincentive for educators to take students with disabilities.

Yet years of research point consistently to the superior outcomes for children, youth, and adults with disabilities when integrated into schools, community-based independent living, competitive employment, and public transportation. The continued organization and efforts of the Disability Rights Movement assures us that these gains will not be lost, even in climates of high-stakes testing and centrally prescribed and regulated curricula.

STUDENT TEACHERS AS COAUTHORS

Knowing little to nothing about the Disability Rights Movement, or even inclusive education, five student teachers accepted my invitation to join a special study group on inclusion and to do their student teaching in inclusive classrooms. I had been running this group for a number of years within the context of the Preservice Master's Program in Elementary Education at Teachers College. We spent an academic year together, meeting weekly, accompanied by Britt Hamre, a doctoral student, who became their student teaching supervisor.

Our method was simple: I brought food, they brought questions and we worked to understand the situation of special education, general education, and inclusion in New York City, and to carefully unpack our own development as teachers. (The use of the first person plural is meant as no fiction here, but rather reflects the genuine questions I brought to the table as a teacher educator, learning alongside my students.)

Early on in our work together I proposed the idea of organizing our oral inquiries around a book project. I recall they all looked at me incredulously, "Could we really write a book?" they asked. And, even now, as this book is almost ready to go to press and emails are sent out with last-minute reference checks and permission forms, they still write back, "I can't believe this is really going to happen!"

Indeed, how many books by student teachers do we ever get to read? Occasionally a first-year teacher comes along who keeps excellent journals and her work is turned into book form; yet the voices of student teachers (while they are student teaching) are rarely heard. Of course there are good reasons for this; primarily we keep them so busy they don't know how they survived the year at all!

Thinking back to our year together, the image that sticks in my mind's-eye is of the sheer diligence, strength, and determination this group brought to the task of learning to be teachers. On the surface, they looked very diverse: Black, White, Asian, Arab, male and female. Yet, once the conversations got going the diversity quotient only increased; it turned out we had a group of students willing to do the hard moral and intellectual work of becoming classroom teachers for all students.

During the year we were writing this book, the student teachers often worried, "Who are we to write a book and tell anyone anything? We are just starting out; we know so little." I reassured them that other student teachers would appreciate reading their inquiries in seminars or in courses that take up issues of elementary education. Since that time, I've had the opportunity to meet with experienced teachers who found the book valuable for its perspective on both inclusion and on the points-of-view of student teachers.

OVERVIEW OF THE BOOK

Chapter 1 details the contexts in which this book was written: the formation of the Inclusive Study Group, situated within an elementary master's teacher education program and the changes in New York City's special education services delivery model; the context of "inclusive education"—whose meaning must always be explained, rather than assumed; and the context of teacher education taken up as situated philosophical, moral, and political inquiry, rather than techno-rational implementation. This former approach to teacher education starts with questions, rather than answers. It situates learning to teach as on-going, recursive, and resistant of formulas. From this stance toward teacher education, there are no "best practices" that can be always and unilaterally recommended. Rather, different practices have different outcomes with different learners. And the teacher must make difficult decisions about curriculum and instruction, often inventing new approaches to unique problems. To support this approach to inquiry-based teacher education, we have included questions at the end of chapters 2–7 that can be used for discussion and also for mini-inquiries in the field.

The student teachers in this volume certainly embraced an inquiry stance to education. Each of the five central chapters of the book is written by an individual student teacher and tracks a specific question over the course of two semesters. The first one, by Carine Allaf, entitled, "My Search for the Perfect Classroom" paints two vivid and contrasting portraits of classrooms that use different models of inclusion. The first classroom is designed with the "consulting teacher" approach: The special educator spends time in the general education classroom working (in this case) with the students with disabilities. In Carine's second placement she student taught in a school that has two teachers in every classroom: one special educator and one general educator. Seeing vast differences between these two classrooms, Carine's chapter critically analyzes how much these changes are about the models used, versus the overall orientations of the teachers toward issues of community, difference, and normalcy. Although some of the stories Carine relates are quite painful, this chapter shines a bright light on small exclusionary moments that many of us might want to turn away from. Carine forces us to look and listen.

"How Teachers Foster Peer Relationships" (chap. 3) by Barbara Wang takes up where Carine leaves off. Specifically, Barbara humorously scrutinizes the central role teachers play in helping children become part of the classroom community. She tells stories (that always made us laugh) about individual children who offer immense challenge to new teachers' commitment to including *all* students. Barbara organizes her chapter around the recognition that teachers must help their students develop strong peer relationships and that the establishment of classroom community is central to working with children who present challenges to authority, patience, and creativity.

As any student teacher will tell you, issues of classroom management often top the list of early and pressing concerns. Many student teachers' postobservation conferences with supervisors circle back to matters of maintaining order. "Investigating the Challenge of Managing a Classroom Full of Individuals," follows Scott Howard as he comes to term with being an authority figure with young children. Inviting us into his classroom with richly drawn tales of his own dilemmas, chapter 4 focuses on the complexities of coming to know so many unique individuals all at once. Scott does not pretend it was easy or that he was always successful, but he challenges us to stay with the questions.

Leslie Gore, in her chapter titled, "Designing Accessible Instruction," carefully details her efforts to plan learning activities that provided success and challenge for all learners regardless of prior skill level. Although much has been written about the need to design such instruction, this may be the very first scholarship documenting a preservice teacher's self-study of her efforts. Chapter 5 avoids the mistakes of much writing on heterogeneous instruction and brings us almost immediately into the microplanning and microteaching of particular lessons. We listen in as Leslie puzzles through instructional dilemmas and cheer with her as they produce learning for both the children and the student teacher.

"Struggle and Change in School Communities," was a difficult chapter for Jen Lee to write. And it may also turn out to be a difficult chapter for readers to encounter. Chapter 6 takes us to the school and community level as Jen investigates the obstacles to creating inclusive schools. Not one to shy away from philosophical questions, Jen challenges us to ask, "What are schools for? What kind of society do we want?" And most tellingly, "What are we as teachers going to do about it?'

Chapter 7 offers a new perspective on what can be learned from student teaching through the eyes of Britt Hamre, a doctoral student who supervised Carine, Barbara, Scott, Leslie, and Jen. In her chapter, "Scaffolding Student Teachers' Inquiries: The Vision in Supervision," it is easy to see how Britt scaffolded the learning of each student teacher and in sophisticated and gentle ways helped them pose the questions that frame their inquiries in this book. Pulling no punches about some of the struggles these student teachers faced, Britt's chapter offers questions that will help all student teachers as they negotiate their sometimes contradictory roles as guests in cooperating teachers' classrooms.

The final chapter, "Being an Inclusive Teacher" addresses the connections among the student teachers' inquiries. Throughout the chapters, the student teachers can be seen developing a firm commitment to a capacity or competency perspective on learners. This is detailed more fully in this last chapter, along with an analysis from a disability studies/disability rights perspective on how inclusion fits into a social (rather than a medical) model of disability.

The authors of this book all believe in possibilities and seek to contribute to conversations that place advocacy, inquiry, contestation, and challenge at the center of the teacher's role. We do not want to be alone in our efforts and dialogues. This volume is our bid for a larger conversation about the challenges of, and necessity for, becoming inclusive teachers. We invite you to join us.

ACKNOWLEDGMENTS

There are numerous family, colleagues, cooperating teachers, and friends who have supported all of us throughout the last few years while we were at Teachers College, and continued to do so as five of us moved on to our first teaching positions. We will not thank all of them here; you know who you are and we would not be where we are without you.

We want to specifically thank three Teachers College students for their timely and important contributions to this volume: Rebekkah Hogan, Edwin Mayorga, and Manisha Ratkalkars. We also deeply appreciate the teachers at Kodak Park School No. 41, in Rochester, New York, who read our entire manuscript and told us how it is also a book that inservice teachers—particularly cooperating teachers—will appreciate reading.

We are indebted to our two reviewers Douglas Biklen and Curt Dudley-Marling who provided extensive and helpful feedback to us not once, but twice! Our work has been strengthened by their generous insights and gentle challenges.

Finally, we want to give a big shout out to the editorial team at Lawrence Erlbaum Associates: Naomi Silverman—editor extraordinaire; her most efficient and friendly assistant, Erica Kica, and our aptly named production editor, Sondra Guideman.

—Celia Oyler

Chapter 1

Learning to Teach in Heterogeneous Elementary Classrooms

Celia Oyler

Starting new things brings both trepidation and excitement. Recently, while accompanying a preservice teacher to her new student teaching placement, we took a shortcut through a city park to get from the university to the yellow brick, three-story elementary school. On the way, she tentatively confided in me about the nervous feeling in her stomach as she began this new venture. I nodded in agreement, "It's always hard to walk into a new place and get to know your way around in a community of strangers."

Such a collection of strangers—five student teachers, their university supervisor, and me, their professor—began meeting one Tuesday afternoon in early September. What brought us together was an articulated commitment to teaching inclusively; although at the time we started, we meant different things by saying we were interested in becoming inclusive teachers. This book was written throughout their year of student teaching and was mostly finished before all the members of the Preservice Inclusion Study Group had secured their first teaching positions.

We formed what some have termed a community of practice (Lave & Wenger, 1991), in our case the Preservice Study Group on Inclusion, and decided early on in our venture together to collect our inquiries as a book. Thus, our weekly 1-hour meetings throughout the school year were organized around first defining, and then conducting topic-focused inquiries centered around the inclusion of students with disabilities in general education classrooms. As we came to know more about each other—as students, as student teachers, and as university-based teacher educators—we also grappled with the various meanings and manifestations of schooling practices that fall under the general term of "inclusion."

We discovered early on that we shared a broad—rather than a narrow—understanding of inclusion. That is, in addition to our commitments to teach children with disabilities alongside their typical peers, we also understand inclusion to mean that teachers see their students as members of various other groups as well: racial, ethnic, gendered, socioeconomic, religious, linguistic, and political. We strive to design curriculum and instruction so that all members of the classroom community are visible and valued—not despite their differences, but with their differences.

This version of inclusion asks teachers to not be "color-blind" (Irvine, 2003), but to understand how children's racial and ethnic identities can be taken up in ways that promote social justice. For example, to say to a colleague, "When I look at Lashandra I don't notice that she's African American," is a denial of not only the historic marginalization and segregation of Black people in the United States, but a failure to understand how learning and teaching are cultural practices. Teachers must therefore be knowledgeable about the ways that African Americans are portrayed in mainstream media, how some children speak African American English and perhaps use more episodic narrative styles (Champion, 2003), and the ways that racism affects various members of many Black communities still today. (And this list is just a small piece of the knowledge that is required to be a culturally competent and responsive teacher.)

Likewise, to teach children with disabilities alongside their typical peers requires teachers to acknowledge the learner's differences, and do so in a way that preserves the dignity and worth of each classroom member. Yet, such teaching, which foregrounds difference, runs contrary to many long-held societal assumptions. For example, many children—and thus many preservice teachers—learn at a very young age that it is not "nice" to notice difference. Think of the young child who points to a man in a wheelchair and asks, "Daddy, what's wrong with him?" The father, because he too was taught not to call attention to difference, completes the learning circle and replies, "Shhh, it's not polite to stare."

When asked to explore assumptions, values, and biases around an issue of race, class, gender, disability, or sexuality one student teacher wrote this recollection in her autobiographical analysis paper:

> In elementary school, Bettina, my classmate was paralyzed from the waist down and used crutches to move around. She was also a child with significant intellectual disabilities. She did not spend much time in our classroom: never came to math, reading, writing, or gym. She did not even lunch with the rest of the class. I remember during the first week of third grade wondering where Bettina disappeared to after 11:00 in the morning. She was part of our classroom for a few hours each day and then seemed to have vanished. When we asked where Bettina was, our teacher responded: "Don't worry about it. It doesn't concern you." I soon stopped wondering why Bettina didn't get to go

on field trips or eat lunch with the rest of the class. I quickly learned that the correct response to difference was to turn the other way and avoid it at all costs.

By becoming inclusive classroom teachers, we seek to create classroom communities where Bettina does not disappear, and where Bettina and all students are both supported and challenged. This requires a very sophisticated pedagogy: one that provides no ceiling, and no floor. This requires an open-ended curriculum that does not pigeon-hole learners in categories that are meant to define them, but leaves the door open to differential academic, emotional, and social growth.

As anyone who has spent any time in classrooms can tell you, there is no class where everyone is on the same level. Whatever the dimension of analysis (gross motor performance, artistic skills, social interactions and decision making, to reading, and writing, and mathematics), all classroom teachers can expect a wide range of skill development. As one inclusive kindergarten teacher said to me in an interview when asked to talk about her reasons for developing multilevel instruction, "Everyone's on a different level, they just don't make people any other way!"

DEVELOPING THE INCLUSION STUDY GROUP

In an effort to contribute to increasing the inclusion of students in the New York City Schools, each year I invited the elementary education master's students who were interested in inclusion to join a discussion/study group that met across both semesters of student teaching. Concurrently, they were placed in inclusive classrooms in various New York City public schools. (Since the writing of this book, New York City has dramatically expanded its number of inclusive classrooms and now more of our program's approximately 75 to 100 placements are in inclusive settings.)

Early on in our year together this extraordinary group of five took up my suggestion to write a book together. With more than 25 years experience as a teacher, I have come to understand the power of authentic products in both shaping and sharpening the learning process. Particularly in collaborative efforts, I have found that a specific end product keeps the group focused and motivated, and is an excellent vehicle for prompting the necessary discussions about process and content. This is certainly true for teacher-research, which is supported by sharing written and oral reports of inquiries with other educators (Cochran-Smith & Lytle, 1993; Goswami & Stillman, 1987; Hubbard & Power, 1999).

Our method was simple. We met for an hour each week, Britt (the doctoral student and student teaching supervisor) and I brought food (as the meetings were at 5:00 p.m. one semester and at 12:45 p.m. the next), we dragged chairs into a circle in my office, and we talked. We rotated responsibility for taking notes on our group conversations, but often engaged in individual, quiet writing, and occasionally viewed a videotape in my collection. Mostly, we told stories, posed questions about particular children or specific practices, asked for advice, or vented our frustrations at what we saw in the field.

Our elementary teacher education program is heavily oriented toward inquiry and reflective practice, and the tone of our meetings was resonant with that. Rarely, then, did student teachers arrive at our Tuesday meetings with questions they expected could be definitively answered. Rather, we engaged in long-winded, passionate dialogues that answered questions with further questions. The spirit in the room, however, was one of support, rather than critique. Indeed, in the process of our work together we have come to see that we all place *community* at the center of our work. That is, we all agree that the formation and nurturance of a community spirit is essential to our work as both inclusive teachers and teacher-researchers. As members of the inclusion study group we have formed a supportive web of relationships that sustain us in the inquiries we report on in this book; so too, as classroom teachers we understand the full inclusion of all students in classroom learning activities to hinge on the establishment of interdependent relationships among students that cross class, gender, race, linguistic, ethnic, religious, and disability lines (Sapon-Shevin, 1999).

AN INQUIRY STANCE WHILE LEARNING TO TEACH

In coming together to write this book we are in agreement that we write from a position of questioning, rather than answering. As Scott put it, "We're not saying, 'this is it, we have the answers.' Rather, we are saying, 'Come listen to the journeys we took during a school year as we came to inquire deeply into our experiences of learning to teach and learning from teaching.' " In each of the chapters our aim is to lend insight into the experience of becoming a teacher from the angle of the student teacher. We write, then, not to tell others what to do, or even to tell others what to believe, but rather, we write to make sense of our "early pilgrimages" (Tomlinson, Callahan, Eiss, Imbeau, & Landrum, 1997) as inclusive teachers.

Each of the student teachers has organized her or his chapter around a particular inquiry question or focus. In a wonderfully serendipitous way, each of our first round of chapter choices fit beautifully together; we selected these themes in early December which allowed the student teachers to tailor some of their spring semester's inquiries around their focusing question. In this way, some of the material for the individual chapters is drawn from papers and projects that were required as part of the student teaching program. Another main source of material has been the student teaching journal required of every student teacher in our program. This is a daily reflective journal read and commented on by their fieldwork supervisor. In writing these chapters, the journals (which were sometimes viewed as burdensome busy-work) proved to be invaluable sources for information regarding the changes in thinking that took place over the course of this school year.

Those changes in thinking and practice, ideas and action, philosophy and implementation are what we seek to highlight in this volume. Student teaching is most surely a journey of discovery, a process of thinking, re-thinking, experimentation, observation, planning, and much pondering. Yet most accounts of student teaching are filtered through the lenses and analysis of teacher educators; rarely do student teachers have the privilege to share their trials and tribulations with a wider audience. In the sharing that we undertake here, we have been persistent in our efforts to unearth the ongoing process of learning to teach. That is, we do not want to present stories from the field as stories conveying even tentative truths set out to tempt the reader to believe us. Rather, we want to uncover the range of emotions and thoughts that swirl around student teachers as they strive to make meaning of their often overwhelming experiences. We share these reflections and inquiries not to provide solutions to the dilemmas of inclusive schooling—the student authors often asked themselves while writing this book, "Who are we to give answers when we are just starting out as teachers?" Instead, we write to invite the reader into the uncertain dilemmas of learning to teach all children.

Viewing teaching as a moral endeavor filled with uncertain and inevitable dilemmas positions the teacher always as an inquirer. In discussing the view of student teaching presented in the preceding paragraph, the coauthors of this book wondered how different actual full-time teaching will be. "Won't these uncertainties, questions, and dilemmas be with us throughout our teaching career?" they queried. "Don't you think you should link this back to teaching and say that this journey through not-knowing is a necessary journey? That being able to learn about yourself is a central aspect of teaching? Isn't teaching an experience that must be embodied like Leslie wrote about in her chapter? That we just have to do it and feel all the emotions that come up and sort through all the tensions and make our sense of the messiness and difficulties?"

It is important to communicate how much we enjoyed our time together while compiling this book. We spent part of May, all of June, and part of July meeting twice a week for 2 hours at a time sharing drafts of our chapters. We conferenced in various pairs and threesomes, we shared references, we told stories that would help others fill in gaps in their chapters, we posed questions to each other, we designed an organizational approach to our chapters to lend textual unity. Therefore, this volume has been crafted in a community of thinkers and writers: a community committed to the possibilities that schools can make a difference not only in the lives of children, but in the future of our democratic practices; a community that believes we are stronger together than alone.

STUDENT TEACHERS NEGOTIATE THEIR ROLES

Student teaching must be understood as one of the most challenging experiences in one's entire teaching career. You arrive in the classroom with all sorts of hopes and dreams about what kind of teacher you will be, but you never really get to fully explore your own approaches as you are a guest in a "borrowed classroom" (Rodriquez, 1998). Very early on in the placement your dreams start to clash with reality when you find not only that teaching is enormously exhausting and mentally demanding, but that your best laid plans are often a disappointment to your cooperating teacher, not quite right for the students, or deemed entirely ineffective by you. What could be so hard about getting 25 students in from recess?

To add to this mix of rude awakenings, students in teacher education programs also have to contend with a society that undervalues teaching and teachers, and with parents and friends who seem to continually question, "Why are you spending so much time and money on becoming a teacher?" It becomes harder and harder to explain to people how much you realize you must learn in this teacher education program and how incredibly difficult you are finding it.

A major challenge throughout student teaching is finding what roles you can play in this borrowed classroom. Much of this, of course, depends on the relationship you have established with your cooperating teacher, and her/his view of what a student teacher should be. The chapters in this book shed light on the various functions student teachers can take on. The traditional understanding of the student teaching role is that of *apprentice.* That is, the student teacher is placed in someone's version of a "model" classroom and the cooperating teacher acts as the exemplar and coach; the job of the student teacher is to imitate the cooperating teacher, and success is viewed as faithfully reproducing the *master* teacher's practices. The terms here—*master* and *apprentice*—come from the craft guilds of the Middle Ages, when young boys were apprenticed to master craftsmen and did increasingly more complex tasks until they fully learned the craft.

Since teaching can certainly be viewed at least in part as a craft, this approach to teacher education has been embraced for nearly a century wherever student teachers are found. Yet over the years, criticisms have been raised of this apprenticeship model, and many teacher educators are pondering the question, "What makes a good student teaching placement?" (Cochran-Smith, 1991; Kroll, LaBoskey, & Richert, 2002; Rust & Koerner, 2002). If teaching is viewed as more than just a series of practices—such as you would find in a skilled craftsperson—then what should be the role of the student teacher?

This issue of deciding where to place student teachers is one fraught with tension for many teacher educators, and also for the students in the program. "Why," recently pleaded one student teacher to me, "aren't we placed in schools with children who really need us?" In exploring her question further, I came to understand that what drew her to teaching was her desire to make a difference in the world by teaching poor students of color in an underresourced school. I explained to her our philosophy on this: As a student teacher, your job is to learn to be the very best teacher you can be; we do not consider that you have the skills to make a meaningful difference in school situations where the teachers are struggling with systemic problems. We do place student teachers in schools where the students are immigrant children, are eligible for free lunch, are considered "high-needs" districts, or are children of color. However, all our schools and teachers are carefully chosen to provide a focus on reflective teaching, rather than mere day-to-day survival.

That said, it must be explained that in the year this book was written, a number of student teaching placements were made in pilot inclusive classrooms. As is visible from the student teachers' inquiries (particularly Carine Allaf's—chapter 2), the teachers themselves had not worked out many of the structural or ideological barriers to full inclusion of students with disabilities. It must be understood from the outset that inclusion does not just mean putting children with and without disabilities together in classrooms. To be fully included in the learning community of a classroom requires sophisticated attention to pedagogy: including a focus on social-emotional issues, a plan for all instructional activities to challenge and support all learners (Kluth, Straut, & Biklen, 2003; Oyler, 2001; Peterson & Hittie, 2003), a willingness to deal directly with children's questions about differential treatment, and the courage to talk explicitly about human difference.

By designing our teacher education program around critical reflection and sustained inquiry, the faculty seek to expand and deepen the roles student teachers can play. While reading these student teachers' inquiries you will notice the shifts they go through as they seek to position and re-position themselves in their cooperating teachers' classrooms. Spending so much time in someone else's classroom is an exceedingly intimate act; and in the intimacy that often develops between student teacher and cooperating teacher it is often a struggle to know what balance to strike in regard to criticism. Although the teacher education program asks for almost continual

reflection and analysis we also require that students seek to understand
the teacher's decisions, rather than simply to judge and then accept or re-
ject these decisions. This stance—of critical analyzer rather than judge—is,
of course, an enormous challenge to take on, while simultaneously taking
on the learning of an entire profession, craft, art, science, and ethic of
teaching.

Yet the student teachers in this book—and I suspect the majority of student teachers in schools across the world—are exceedingly capable of negotiating and re-negotiating multiple and shifting roles as they learn to
teach. Leslie Gore, for example, in her chapter demonstrates the role of the
student teacher who realizes—in the flash of one moment—that she can
bring practices of multilevel instruction into her student teaching classroom and thus act as an agent of transformation rather than just technical
reproduction. As her lesson on time demonstrates, she experiments with a
form of pedagogy that had not been modeled and suddenly sees the potential to grow into a student teaching role that brings new practices into the
classroom.

THE STUDENT TEACHERS' PROGRAM
AND ASSIGNMENTS

The work the student teachers engaged in during the course of the year,
and indeed in the writing of this book, can be understood as a form of
teacher research or teacher inquiry. Preservice teacher education programs across the English-speaking world are asking their students to engage in systemic inquiry into children, youth, communities, schools, and
teaching/learning as a formalized aspect of learning to teach. This move is
paralleled (and even initiated) by an extensive body of research and inquiry
conducted by teachers in order to generate knowledge and understanding
about practices, theories, and contexts of teaching and learning.

This move toward research and inquiry *by* teachers—not about them, on
them, for them, or even with them—must be understood as fundamentally
altering the power relationships inherent in knowledge about teachers and
their ways of working. For much of the 20th century, university experts attempted to corner the market on research about teaching and learning.
With the move away from normal schools (where women teachers and principals had been the primary instructors) as the sites of teacher education,
and toward schools and colleges of education, teachers became increasingly distanced from the knowledge generated about them and supposedly
for them (Gitlin, 2000). Therefore, the move toward teacher-initiated and
controlled research and inquiry can be seen as a political movement with
implications for the future of teachers and teaching. Rather than knowl-

edge about teaching being conferred from an outside expert, teacher research positions teachers to "construct Knowledge (with a capital K) about teaching, learning, and schooling" (Cochran-Smith & Lytle, 1993, p. 43).

This is a move with enough potential influence and power that it is contested. Take, for example, the debate about if teacher research should really count as *research*. Although an enormous array of articles and books abound that are the result of teacher inquiries, some academics are still debating the value of these inquiries as contributing to a wider knowledge base about teaching (Anderson & Herr, 1999; Cochran-Smith, 1990; Wong, 1995). However contested the terrain, the arena of teacher research, and even preservice teacher inquiry is well mapped out (Clandinin, Davies, Hogan, & Kennard, 1993; Cochran-Smith, 2004; Cochran-Smith & Lytle, 1993; Duckworth, 1997; Hollingsworth, 1994; Pappas & Zecker, 2001a, 2001b; Poetter, 1997; Teel & DeBruin-Parecki, 2001; Wells, 2001) and our teacher education program has benefited from this tradition.

Briefly, we integrate teacher inquiry into these major projects:

1. The first semester all student teachers engage in a "Child Inquiry" that entails a wide range of data collection strategies seeking to closely observe a particular child over the course of a semester in a wide variety of contexts (Goodwin, 2002). Preservice teachers are encouraged to revise any initial assumptions previously made based on these close observations and to consider what children are communicating through their behavior.

2. Also during the first semester, all student teachers develop a question they explore through published research. Many of the research references throughout this book were generated in the context of writing these inquiries into "what does the published research say?"

3. During the second semester preservice teachers are required to conduct a "School Inquiry." In this project, student teachers identify three specific questions about some aspect of the school organization. Categories for investigation include: the school-wide learning environment; school-wide decision making and communication; the school as a workplace for adults (teachers, staff, administrators); and school–community relationships (parents, families, community organizations, and so forth).

In writing their chapters, the authors of this book were able to use these and other assignments from the preservice program. As noted previously, the authors of this volume have also drawn heavily on their student teaching journals that were kept as a requirement for the program. You will notice throughout the chapters that reflection and analysis of data and experiences has played a central role in these teachers' journeys. Such an orientation does seek opinions and knowledge from "experts" such as researchers, more experienced teachers, professors, and university supervisors, but even more importantly, this orientation toward learning to teach seeks to filter all knowledge and experiences through critical inquiry. This style of critical inquiry begins with a deep analysis of our own assumptions, biases, perspectives, and worldviews.

Our program asks student teachers to do this sort of inquiry into their own consciousness. What do we assume about children, their parents, their neighborhoods, and their "abilities" based on our own experiences growing up? How have our own school, family, and community experiences shaped us to understand the world? What are some of our ways of knowing that are culturally framed? And then, most significantly, what might we do as teachers to speak back to the cultures that have helped shape us and lend sense to our ways of understanding the world? These critical autobiographical analyses are organized into two major papers written at the beginning of each semester, and are also included in the student teaching/program portfolios submitted at the end of each semester.

Although the areas of race, class, gender, sexual orientation, and religion figure prominently in the discourses of critical and multicultural teacher education (Cochran-Smith, 2004; Darling-Hammond, French, & Garcia-Lopez, 2002; Irvine, 2003) disability is often left without interrogation. This can be partially explained by the dual system of special education and general education that has resulted in most U.S. teachers never having developed a close friendship with someone with a disability. Because of segregated employment options, such as sheltered workshops, adults rarely encounter coworkers with disabilities. This social segregation is then reinforced by teacher education programs (such as the one these student teacher authors attended) that prepare those to be certified in special education separately from all general education programs.

Limited contact with peers with disabilities places inclusive classroom teachers at a distinct disadvantage, when it comes to having children with disabilities in the classroom. As one student teacher (not an author of this book) wrote in her first autobiographical analysis paper:

> I ask myself, "How do I look at people in wheelchairs, with physical deformities, [*sic*] or disabling diseases? Do I consider these people a part of the society in which I live?" Reflecting, I realize that while I am accepting of differences, I take little action to understand and support those with disabilities. I do not stare, I do not judge, and I, in turn, do not do anything. In my life this far, I have made little effort to change the negative manner in which most of society views the physically disabled. I fear teaching students with cognitive and physical disabilities. I need experience with the unknown, and I must face the unfamiliar.

The authors of this book all shared this student's commitment to face the unknown and lean toward—rather than shying away from—the unfamiliar.

Each of the authors of this volume asks, "*How* can I best include students with disabilities in my classroom?" rather than the more typical question: "*Which* students do I want to include?" Most, but not all, of the cooperating teachers with whom these student teachers worked, also asked the "how," rather than the "which" question about inclusion. This must be understood against the backdrop of special education in New York City.

INCLUSION IN NEW YORK CITY

It is often said about education, schools, and teaching that "context is everything"; perhaps this is true of any human endeavor. So to understand some of the experiences these preservice teachers encountered during student teaching, it is important to explain a bit about the context of schools in New York City, particularly in regard to inclusion. During the year these student teachers wrote their chapters (2001–2002) New York City public school-teachers were in their second year without a contract. This meant a frozen pay scale and an increasing number of teachers drawn to the surrounding suburbs in search of a livable wage; New York City was about 15% behind its neighboring districts in regard to teacher salaries.

Special education in the city was in its first year of implementing "The New Continuum." A source of much tension, misunderstanding, and top-down decrees, this new continuum of services was put into place when the federal government threatened New York State with a loss of nearly $325 million in special education monies. New York City has a severe over-representation of African American and Latino students in self-contained special education placements and was deemed severely out of compliance with the least restrictive environments mandates of the law passed some 25 years ago mandating special education services (PL 94-142). This "New Continuum of Services" attempted to bring more students from segregated self-contained special education classrooms into general education. Yet teachers were often underprepared for such inclusion and viewed the newly integrated students with suspicion and fear.

New York City has a two-tiered special education system. The 32 Community School Districts that are spread across Manhattan, Brooklyn, Queens, The Bronx, and Staten Island provide special education services to students formally labeled with the term Moderate Intervention Services (MIS). Students with more significant disabilities are taught in an entirely separate school district: New York Citywide Special Education School District #75. This segregated school district has approximately 19,000 children and youth taught in either self-contained special education school buildings or in self-contained special education programs located in general education schools with extra space. Not surprisingly, the District 75 programs can sometimes still be found in obscure corners of the buildings—segregated off to the side. Some of the elementary education student teachers who were not part of the inclusion group expressed grim surprise when they discovered these tucked-away classrooms during the spring semester school inquiry projects.

District 75 also runs an inclusion program, in which a small but dedicated staff works to broker deals with individual principals across the 32 community school districts. There are built-in disincentives to take students from District 75 as New York City is also pressuring principals and school districts to obtain higher scores on city and state high-stakes tests. To comply with federal laws, students with IEPs must be tested with these criterion-referenced (state tests) and norm-referenced (city tests) measures of what people persist in terming "achievement." This mandate to include students with disabilities in group achievement tests can be traced to a fine motive: Let's hold all students to high standards and give students with disabilities access to the general education curriculum. Indeed the reauthorization of the Individuals with Disabilities Education Act Amendments of 1997 requires that special education students be provided with access to the general education curriculum. The specific rub in New York City's inclusion efforts, however, is that to qualify for special education services in the first place, you must receive at least a few low scores on achievement tests (otherwise you aren't eligible for services). So for principals to take on an inclusion program with District 75 students means they are signing up for potentially lower achievement test scores. At the same time, just contemplate what a gifted and talented program could net a building administrator in terms of scores!

FOSTERING INCLUSIVE CLASSROOM TEACHING

Yet, despite these massive, systemic challenges to inclusion and equity, there are numerous schools throughout New York City quite valiantly taking the lead to open their doors to all neighborhood children—even those with disabilities. Various models are being used: collaborative full-time team teaching, and part-time consulting teacher services being the two most common ones. In her chapter in this book, Carine Allaf explores her contrasting experiences with these two models and analyzes the effects these approaches had on both classroom teachers as well as students.

The inclusion study group for preservice teachers grew out of a long-term collaboration I had with members of the Think Tank on Unified and Equitable Education. This was a group of administrators and teachers who met together to plan and implement pilot inclusive programs merging services and students from one community school district and students from the special education district. We also developed ways to increase the number of educators prepared to teach in inclusive classrooms. Our project to build and support inclusive classrooms in New York City is predicated on the understanding that the very mechanisms that help support students with disabilities to be fully included, successful, and challenged in general education classrooms, also provide necessary elements to more adequately meet the needs of students without labeled disabilities.

For example, in successful inclusive classrooms you will find: (a) flexible groupings that change with the purpose of the group and are not fixed or determined by someone's notion of a learner's "ability"; (b) instruction that is inherently multilevel (Peterson & Hittie, 2003; Peterson, Tamor, Feen, & Silagy, 2002) and offers a wide range of learners opportunities to acquire skills, explore content, and develop conceptual understanding, *even if those skills, content and concepts might not be the exact same ones*; and (c) explicit attention to building a community of learners with open acknowledgment of student differences (Sapon-Shevin, 1999) and continual teacher attention to equalizing status differences (Cohen, 1994). These three factors must be understood as beneficial and important to all learners, not just students with IEPs.

Learning to teach using community-building, multilevel instruction, and flexible instructional groups is certainly a complex endeavor. Although these ideas are supported by a large number of teacher educators, little research exists that explores the issues preservice teachers and their teacher educators face as they engage in this project. Although much literature exhorts teachers about what to do to support the inclusion of students with disabilities in general education, few studies have taken up the issue of inclusive teacher education directly. Thus, in support of this line of inquiry, we engaged in ongoing sustained self-study as we progressed through the year together in the Preservice Inclusion Study Group.

As we worked together to finalize our book, and we read our texts next to, and with each other, we saw our shared commitment that frames this book. It is a commitment we had not articulated until we read our words on the pages. We all noticed it and commented on it. That is, we share a strong commitment to critiquing the status quo. Along with many other preservice teachers (Darling-Hammond et al., 2002) we want schools and communities, and indeed our nation and world to be a better place. Yet we are not content to merely critique. We understand the responsibility that has come with the obvious privileges we hold. As teachers and community members, as teacher-researchers and writers, we seek to build on our critique and take an active role in transforming our classrooms, schools, neighborhood, nation, and world. We choose to engage in this daunting endeavor collectively, and invite you along on one of our first such ventures.

Chapter 2

Carine Allaf's Inquiry: My Search for the Perfect Classroom

A couple of weeks after sending in my deposit to attend Teachers College, Columbia University to pursue my Master of Arts in Elementary Education, I received a packet of papers to fill out. Flipping through the various papers, one green sheet immediately caught my eye. On the very top were the words, *Think Tank on Unified and Equitable Education.* The explanation mentioned student teaching in an inclusive classroom, but at this point I had no idea what inclusion meant and proceeded to read the green paper in order to find out more. On a whim, I decided to sign up for this extra work and sent in the form.

As September approached I started receiving numerous emails detailing information on student teaching placements, orientation, and housing. In the midst of this rush of emails I received one that congratulated me on being part of the *Think Tank on Unified and Equitable Education.* I had no clue what that was or how I got sent that email. I did not remember that green piece of paper from May. As I walked to the first inclusion meeting of the year, I did not know what to expect or what this year would have in store for me.

WHAT IS NORMAL?

I did not realize that inclusion could and would appear to me in two very different forms. I also did not know how quickly I would become passionate about inclusion. Both of my student teaching placements were labeled as "inclusive settings," yet my experiences in both classrooms barely resembled

14

each other. This chapter details my journey in two extremely different inclusive classrooms. Throughout this journey with inclusion I observed a variety of factors and attitudes coming from, and influenced by, the adults in these two inclusive settings. I constantly posed various questions (which are the focus of this chapter) in order to gain a better understanding of inclusion, how it works, and what a fully inclusive environment looks like. Why did it appear to be so different in my two student teaching placements? What made each class run as it did? What worked and what did not work and why? How were children affected by the infrastructures put in place by both the schools and the teachers? In what way does the model of inclusion that a school follows affect the children's and school's relationships? How have my student teaching experiences affected my thought processes and decision making in my job search? Although most of my questions were not necessarily answered during my student teaching year, my experiences have helped clarify and solidify a lot of my thoughts, ideas, and opinions.

The Master of Arts program in preservice elementary education at Teachers College requires about four semesters of course work. During two of these four terms we are engaged in full-time student teaching. I decided to complete this program in one year (from one summer to the next) so I took on additional courses during my student teaching semesters. One course proved essential to influencing my understandings about disability and therefore inclusion. The course was titled, "*Disabilities Reconsidered, Reconstructed*" and really opened my eyes to both mainstream society and disability culture and essentially broke down the word "normal." What is normal and how is normalcy perceived by society and why is it perceived that way? The Disability Rights Movement, along with disability culture, have made it no longer acceptable to educate disabled students in self-contained classrooms in the hidden hallways of schools. This move to include special education students has also forced schools to move from a "one size fits all" method of instruction toward a multileveled and differentiated form (which Leslie Gore writes about in chapter 5). I want to emphasize, however, that inclusion is not just the integration of children with disabilities, it's about making sure *no* student gets excluded. After all, every child learns differently. I have come to believe that the responsibility is on us as teachers to structure our teaching styles in order to meet the needs of all their students, labeled or not.

Throughout my teacher education program I often used required papers to pursue questions I wanted to explore in more depth. For my final paper in the "*Disabilities Reconstructed and Reconsidered*" class I undertook an exploration of the two different models of inclusion and how they seemed to affect the outcomes for children. In both my student teaching placements the schools utilized a collaborative approach for the implementation of inclusive programming in their schools.

From reading the educational literature on inclusion and various service delivery models, I was reassured to discover that no one expects a single teacher to be able to meet the needs of all the learners on her own. Rather, it is through a collaborative effort that teachers attempt to meet all the needs of all the children. Collaboration—according to my review of the literature—is described as all members of a school and community working together and supporting each other in a set of interactions to offer the highest quality of instruction for the different types of learners they serve (Stainback & Stainback, 1996). Stanovich (1996) believes that effective collaborative practices take place when general educators experience collaborative relationships with special educators, parents, paraprofessionals, principals, and other related service personnel. Collaboration supports the saying that "two heads are better than one" and is based on the premise that the more school personnel can collaborate to meet the needs of the learners, the better off all students are in that educational setting. Collaboration and community go hand in hand and are critical components of a positive inclusive classroom. These themes are constant and are woven throughout this book as our inquiries into inclusion lead us to believe that educators must work together both *in* the community and to *create* a community.

MY TWO STUDENT TEACHING PLACEMENTS

My first student teaching placement was in a fifth-grade inclusive classroom at Public School 700,[1] a K–5 educational institution. Most classrooms in P.S. 700 are general education classrooms and each grade has approximately one or two inclusive classrooms. This school follows a consulting teaching model of inclusion with a general educator and a special educator moving among several classrooms. Villa and Thousand (2000) describe this method where both the paraprofessional and teacher take part in teaching duties whereby a special education teacher serves as a part-time consultant to two or more general education teachers (Lipsky & Gartner, 1997). This model is based on the assumption that the special educator brings specialized information to a problematic situation (McGregor & Vogelsberg, 1998). The special educator is part of a team with the general educators to ensure that all the students in an inclusive setting are benefiting. The special educator working in my classroom, one of a group of six at the school, was responsible for two fifth-grade and one first-grade classrooms and entered my room approximately three times a week for two 45-minute periods (one in literacy and one in math). In this particular fifth-grade class, approximately 6 of

---

[1]We have used pseudonyms (or pseudonumbers) for all schools, teachers, and children throughout the book.

the 30 students had Individualized Education Plans (IEPs). These students were labeled from emotionally disturbed, to autistic, to learning disabled. P.S. 700 expected the general educator, special educator, and paraprofessional to constantly collaborate in order to meet the needs of the children with disabilities. The general educator and special educator met approximately once a week to sort out their plans.

My second placement was in a first grade at Public School 300, an alliance between a community school district and District 75—special education district in New York City. P.S. 300 is a pre-K to fifth-grade school. At the time they were the only school in New York City to fully integrate special and general education students in every class. Approximately one third of the students in each classroom have special needs as described on an IEP and the other two thirds are general education students. In my classroom, 6 of the 23 students had IEPs. The school follows a full-time, collaborative coteaching model that includes one general educator, one special educator, and one paraprofessional in every classroom. Scott Howard (see chapter 4) and I student taught at the South Campus, which contains approximately 170 students, pre-K to second grade. The other campus, Central, which is the larger of the two, serves 325 students. At both sites, the general and special educators have at least one prep period each day along with lunch to collaborate and plan. Unfortunately, no time is built into the daily schedule for paraprofessionals to participate in this process.

In reflecting on my two different student teaching placements and trying to understand how structures affect classroom dynamics, I must note that there are substantial differences between fifth and first graders, therefore making a simple comparison impossible. These students are at completely different developmental periods in their lives and as a result their behaviors differ tremendously. My intent is to simply illustrate how inclusion presents itself in two very different classrooms, despite the obvious difference in age and curriculum, I have come to see that the structures, routines, and language in any grade level classroom can be compared to explore how they shape the experiences of the children in the school and make the classroom more or less inclusive.

According to Stainback and Stainback (1996) all inclusive schools have the same underlying philosophy: All children can learn and belong in the mainstream of school and community life. The National Study of Inclusive Education in 1994 identified at least eight factors for success: visionary leadership; collaboration; refocused use of assessment; support for staff and students; funding; effective parental involvement; and the implementation of effective program models and classroom practices (Villa & Thousand, 2000). The execution of these eight factors differed tremendously in P.S. 700 and P.S. 300, which is one reason why inclusion appeared to be so different in my two student teaching placements.

Peers Working Together

From the first day of school, the general educator in my fifth-grade placement insisted on placing the labeled students together at a table. She
claimed that this seating arrangement facilitated transition and instruction
when the special educator came in to assist. Right before the winter vacation in December, the general educator switched the classroom assigned
seats. I was excited at the prospect of having all the children get new seats.
As she rearranged the students, she started placing the same special needs
children at that same back table. Before finalizing the new seating arrangement, she asked if anyone was unhappy with their seat and would like to
change. Larry (one of the back-table kids) threw his arm up in the air and
flung his body over his desk in desperation. He wanted to get away from
that dreaded table, from that everlasting label. Finally after much prodding
on both his and my part, Larry got to sit somewhere else with the understanding that he would come to the back table during reading and math. I
cannot describe this boy's facial expression as he moved from the back table to his new seat. He was both elated and relieved.

A few weeks earlier, I heard one of the students that was not labeled special needs exclaim, "That's where the retards sit. I would never want to sit
there." Hearing that comment, I was furious. I contemplated interrupting
the whole class to discuss this inappropriate comment. I wanted to scream
at this child. How can he be so inconsiderate and ignorant? Was it my role,
however, to intervene? Could I teach something to these kids that was not
predetermined by my cooperating teacher? How did I not cross the line between student teacher and teacher? I did not know what to do. I knew, however, that I needed to address this comment in some way. I pulled the child
aside and spoke to him about his comment. I will never forget the boy's reaction. His face seemed to read, "Relax lady, what's the big deal?" I wanted
him to realize the implications of using that word. But after talking to him
about people's strengths and challenges and how that comment could
make people feel I sent him back to his desk. To this day, his comment still
aggravates me. Is this child, however, really the one to blame? After all, his
comment echoed the environment of the classroom. How could he know
any better?

In contrast, in my second placement, students were seated at six tables all
around the room. Every table held a different number of students and the
seating arrangement was very flexible. Each table was labeled a different
color and my cooperating teachers made sure that the seating arrangement
changed at least once every month. One child, Sally, seated at the green table seemed to be constantly getting into fights with the other children at
her table. She was not sharing the pencils, she was hogging the markers, she
was talking too loudly and the other children could not concentrate. After
many days of complaining and tears, Sally approached one of my cooperat-

ing teachers and stated that she did not feel like that table was a good place for her. She needed to move. Immediately the teacher hailed Sally for her mature behavior and asked her where she would prefer to sit. Sally picked a seat at the table adjacent to the green table and after that there were no more complaints, neither from Sally or her new tablemates. This incident made me realize how high these teachers' expectations were for their students, and how well the children rose to meet them. These first graders were expected to monitor their own behavior and make good choices. They were guided to really know themselves and each other, which allowed them to conduct themselves appropriately and as a result build a positive and cohesive classroom environment.

Although children were seated randomly around the room, my cooperating teachers Jackie and Candace tried to keep students seated next to their reading/writing partners. These partnerships were constantly changing to ensure that the same students did not always work with each other. Jackie and Candace based the reading partnerships on the skill levels of the students. For instance, there were some children reading chapter books while others were working on recognizing letters in the alphabet. So in subjects other than reading and writing, teachers constantly tried to pair students they rarely or never work with. From this classroom, I learned to carefully consider partners and groups; for instance, during one of my lessons I asked the students to use a class-made key to map out, in partnerships, one street of the school neighborhood. I purposefully placed students together that I had never seen work together or who had only interacted on rare occasions. For this activity, I did not really consider students strengths and weaknesses in academic subjects but rather just wanted children to broaden their horizons and interact with someone they otherwise would not have talked to. In other lessons, however, I took the time to pair students both according to strengths and challenges and with whom they worked well. For example, John and Ian consistently worked extremely well with each other. During one activity on the 100th day of school, they built an immense structure out of 100 bottle caps. Based on this experience, the following week I paired the two together during a math lesson on polygons. The children were instructed to create polygons using straws and twisty ties. John and Ian were both excited when I called their names together as they both exclaimed "Yessss!" In fact one of the other children, Elizabeth, grinning widely, shared with the class, "I really think Ian and John work well together."

Differentiated Teaching and Children's Awareness of Difference

I am not sure that the children in my fifth-grade placement were aware of the classroom environment they inhabited. For instance, were they aware that they were in an inclusive class? Did they know what that meant? Fur-

thermore, is it even necessary that they know they are in an inclusion setting? Shouldn't a general feeling of acceptance and community take place
in any classroom? Is it necessary that these children know they are in a classroom with special needs children or is it more necessary that they are
taught to care and appreciate everyone in the class, regardless of what class
they are in?

During one of my first lessons as a student teacher, I read to the students
a story about the Cyclops. After reading this story, I allowed the children to
create their own myth using the Cyclops as the main character. After writing the story, the children were asked to illustrate their created mythologi-
cal creatures. As I walked around the room monitoring student work I
stopped by the "special needs" table. Everyone seemed to be working hard,
heads down scribbling away. I start reading one girl's story and realized it
had nothing to do with Greek Mythology but was rather a story about a girl
and her family. Fred seated at the same table across from her just looked at
me and asked, "What's up with her?" This girl, Casey, was obviously very different from the other children. Although I was never allowed to look at her
IEP I was told that she had "a lot of problems" including behaviors similar
to those of children with autism. Casey was 13 years old and had attended
summer school for the past couple years. When Fred posed that question I
suddenly realized that the issue of understanding differences was never addressed in this classroom. Any behavior that deviated from the norm was
immediately criticized not just by the teacher but by the students as well. Although Casey was not completing the required assignment, she was writing
an entertaining and well-thought-out story with a matching and detailed il-
lustration. Although this might appear as slacking or avoiding the work to
other students to the class, I felt that Casey did accomplish something from
that activity. I wondered: Was it absolutely necessary that Casey demonstrates knowledge of mythology or should I be pleased with her accomplishment of storytelling? I do believe that learning did take place during my lesson for Casey although her story did not look like everyone else's. Yet,
through the eyes of the rest of the children and my cooperating teacher,
Casey's story was crazy. "How can a child miss the whole point of the lesson?" I was asked. When I collected all the assignments, my cooperating
teacher photocopied Casey's story in order to show it to her teacher friends
at other schools to prove how "clueless" this child really was.

The second placement gave me an opportunity to see learning centers
created specifically based on the children's strengths and weaknesses. The
teachers designed literacy centers to which children rotated in groups over
a 2-week period. The centers included various activities such as writing
words in sand, using magnetic letters to create words, putting sentence
strips together to make a poem, and word wall bingo. One day in February,
during these centers, one boy Tim complained that he wanted to go to the

sand center. He did not understand why some children got to go to that specific center and he did not. Tim did not realize that he did not need to go to the sand center because his writing skills were very well developed. The teacher just refreshed Tim's memory that this classroom's job is to help everybody become the best student they can be; some students needed different things than other students. Tim was supposed to participate in different centers than other children. He needed different things in order to succeed and be the best student he could be. Tim looked up at the teacher's face, after being told this, clutching his hands together. He simply grinned and said, "Oh yeah! Okay!" and ran off to his center. This small incident demonstrates how much work had taken place at the beginning of the year. Children in this class were expected to understand that all students learn at their own pace and that it is okay if they are not all doing the same learning activities. For my future classroom I must be prepared, however, for kids to be kids, and every once in a while expect students to complain about the activities they are doing in comparison to someone else in the class. A simple conversation, similar to that with Tim, will hopefully clear up any further complaints and refocus the children's attention to the task at hand.

The students in the first-grade class were aware that they were in an inclusive classroom. They understood that everyone in that class possessed different talents and that they all had their own challenges. They openly discussed these similarities and differences and not only understood, but expected differentiated treatment. In contrast, my fifth graders did not possess the same mentality. They believed everybody should be on the same page, doing the same thing. If a child deviated from the norm, then it was a big deal. The fact that everyone in the class was different was never addressed. Although my cooperating teacher tried to treat all the students in the same way to bypass "unfair treatment," students treated each other in distinctly and explicitly different manners.

Coteaching Versus Skill Level Grouping

At P.S. 700 the special educator entered the classroom twice a day at least three times a week to assist with instruction. One prep period a week was specifically designated to allow the general educator time to plan with the special educator. These meetings included my cooperating teacher describing what she planned on teaching that particular day and then the two teachers would decide how to split the class up in order to teach the same lesson in two speeds, regular/advanced and slow. As a result, every lesson the teachers conducted together, they would simply split the class and concentrate on teaching the group they were assigned (general education or special education). In every case, the special educator and paraprofessional were in charge of the "struggling" learners and the general educator and I were to teach those who were "succeeding." Within the two groups, the same instructional practices were used across the board; worksheets, rote memorization, and repetition. No multiple teaching strategies took place. The higher group did more difficult work or progressed at a faster pace, whereas the lower group did the same worksheets and problems but at a slower pace with more assistance and one-on-one attention.

One example of this was the weekly guided reading groups. Both groups read books based on P.S. 700's fifth-grade theme of brotherhood [sic] and friendship. The special educator's group was reading Elizabeth George Speare's The Sign of the Beaver. Using a teacher's guide as reference, the children worked on vocabulary worksheets, quizzes, and short answer assignments during their guided reading sessions. My group and the general educator's group read Theodore Taylor's The Cay. Also using a teacher's guide, I distributed different handouts each day for the children to complete in their small groups. During these guided reading sessions, I noticed that one child was struggling with The Cay. After mentioning this to my cooperating teacher, she glared at the child and said to me with a loud voice, "Well, if it's too hard for her, then she will just have to go with The Sign of the Beaver group!" The teacher's tone of voice and reaction indicated that she regarded reading with The Sign of the Beaver group a punishment while reading The Cay was a reward and a privilege. This child, then, was not being encouraged to be comfortable with her reading level. Rather, she was being pushed to read a book that she might not have been ready to read simply due to a stigma placed on The Sign of the Beaver group.

Rather than having the feeling of one cohesive classroom environment, it felt like there were two groups of learners that were simply being housed in the same classroom. The general education teacher did not deal with any special education children. If phone calls needed to be made about them she would ask the paraprofessional or special education teacher to make them. She would always state that the special needs children "were not her business." In fact, during report cards, the general educator, after filling out the attendance records, gave the special needs children's report cards to the special education teacher to fill out. My cooperating teacher told me that she wouldn't know what to write or what grades to give them. At the beginning of the year, my cooperating teacher told me that she did not look at the children's IEPs and records because she did not want to make any premature judgments. She wanted the students to start out new and not have a file hanging over their heads. I asked her around report card time (early November) if she had looked at the IEPs. She told me that she had not and that she didn't even know where they were. She also said that it wasn't really necessary for her to look at them.

During Guided Reading the special educator would come in and would teach the whole class while my cooperating teacher sat at one of the children's desks and assisted with discipline. During math sessions, the special educator would take a group of children who were struggling with that concept either to the back of the room or in the hall and work with them. One day, Alex was having a very hard time using his protractor to read angles. My cooperating teacher immediately told him to go with the special educator in the hall. Amidst the giggling and ooohing from his classmates, Alex wrinkled his face and quickly looked down at this paper. He then exclaimed, "Oh wait! I get it!!" Later on I walked past Alex's desk and noticed that all his angle measurements were incorrect. In an almost secretive manner, I crouched near his desk and in a whisper helped Alex make sense of his protractor. I do admit I was scared we would get caught and yelled at. My cooperating teacher would have insisted that if Alex did not understand the material then he belonged in the hall with the other children like him. There was no need for him to waste my time or the other children's because he did not understand how to use a protractor.

In contrast to this push-in/consultation model in my fifth-grade classroom, the first-grade class had a special educator with the general educator in the room at all times. Upon walking into the class, however, you could not tell which teacher was which. They both worked with all children during all subjects. During reading and writing workshop times, both teachers, and sometimes the paraprofessional and I, circulated around the room conferencing with various children. The teachers had made a grid that stated each child's name in a small box for conferencing notes. This grid contained three columns and eight rows. The teachers would either cut this strip into three vertical strips or four horizontal ones depending on the number of adults in the room available to conference. These conferencing grids ensured that each teacher got to work with different children every reading/writing workshop. It was, therefore, completely random who was on each teacher's conference list.

During math, Jackie usually conducted the minilessons. Each math lesson (which lasted approximately 10–15 minutes) was followed by a hands-on activity at the children's tables. During this activity time, both teachers, the paraprofessional, and I all walked around the room helping students with the activity. Furthermore, all students were not always responsible for the same type of work. Jackie and Candace many times would modify journal pages in the *Everyday Mathematics* workbooks to fit the needs of the students. For example, one boy who was autistic needed bigger print on his worksheets and according to his IEP needed to work with money in 5-, 10-, and 25-cent denominations. On a money worksheet, the print would be enlarged and the problems would be changed to only include the denomina-

tions Adam needed to work with. Adam was not the only student that
needed modifications in this class. Walking around the class during a lesson, I would see the children all working on the same basic task but in different manners.

Both teachers were also responsible for filling in IEPs and report cards.
Jackie and Candace choose to have one of them fill out the IEP and have
the other proofread and add anything. They believed that this takes less
time and allows for the IEPs to have both of their input. During report card
times, they split the class into two halves. They each fill out one half and
then they trade to read what the other has written and add their comments,
if any. In the third quarter, Jackie had taken the first half of the alphabet
and Candace the second. So in the fourth marking period, Candace filled
out the first half of the alphabet and Jackie did the second half.

Integrating Paraprofessionals Into the Classroom

In my experiences this year, a paraprofessional was present in both of these
inclusive classrooms. When paraprofessionals are present in a New York
City classroom, some are assigned to specific students and others are assigned as general classroom paraprofessionals. It was very difficult for us in
the inclusion study group to find the roles and responsibilities of paraprofessionals but we began to understand the role a bit more from Jennifer
Lee's inquiries (see chapter 6). The two paraprofessionals I interacted with
this past year differed completely in their jobs and demeanor with the children. I wondered how much of this was a result of the different personali-
ties of the two paraprofessionals and how much was a result of the expectations in the two different classrooms? When I think about having my own
classroom and perhaps being assigned a paraprofessional with whom to
work, I realize that I must take a great deal of responsibility for integrating
the paraprofessional into the classroom community.

Dana was the paraprofessional in my fifth-grade student teaching placement. She was fairly young at 26 and has been at P.S. 700 for 2 years. She
was a fifth-grade paraprofessional last year with a different teacher and this
was her first time working with my cooperating teacher. Dana had a very
friendly and close relationship with the children. The students were very interested in Dana's life and always asked her questions about her two small
sons. She was with the class all day, except for lunch and recess. Dana was
designated to work with Casey and Larry, who needed the most instructional assistance according to the special education teacher. As a result,
there was always an empty desk for Dana near both Larry and Casey. Once
Larry was allowed to sit at a different table than Casey and the "special
needs" table, a chair was placed near his desk for Dana. Dana also assisted
with classroom duties such as homework correction and recording, bulletin

boards, and handing out papers but she mainly worked with Larry and Casey. She made sure they wrote down their homework, completed assignments, and conducted themselves properly. Any time phone calls were needed for either Larry or Casey, she made them. If either child got into trouble, Dana dealt with it. The other children in the class could tell that Dana was there to work with those two children, although at times Dana worked with the children that were struggling on one particular topic.

The general educator and paraprofessional sometimes engaged in mocking and making fun of the special needs children. One day, the teacher loudly exclaimed that Casey was getting ready to meet her boyfriend. As I looked over at the student, I noticed that she was engaging in a repetitive behavior of curling one section of her hair. As the class erupted in laughter, Casey did not appear to be attending to what was going on in her classroom and seemed to be captivated in another world. Regardless, this comment made it seem that it was okay to make fun of other people's odd behaviors when in fact, what appears to be odd to us might actually be purposeful to that child.

This general classroom attitude allowed children to constantly approach Dana with other odd behaviors that either Larry or Casey exhibited during times when Dana was not present. They were always coming back from lunch and recess stating, "Dana you won't believe what *she* did today. . . ." One day in late November the class came back from lunch in a very heated manner. A big fight had erupted between Larry and some other boys. My cooperating teacher immediately called the paraprofessional and special educator to deal with Larry's rage. After Larry was calmed down and the details of the fight were straightened out, my cooperating teacher approached Larry and talked to him about fighting in school.

What made communication particularly difficult was that there was no planning time set aside for the teachers to meet with the paraprofessional. Dana would arrive daily about 5 minutes before the children and would leave with the students at dismissal. She would also leave for lunch. As a result, there was no time to really sit down and collaborate with the other educators. Many times, then, Dana did not know what was going to take place during the lesson. The general educator would give her directions either during a lesson or quickly at the beginning of one. Dana was only present during school hours. She did not attend any out of school activities and was not present at open-school night and parent–teacher conferences (unless she was specifically asked to be available for a particular reason).

In my first-grade placement, Linda was the classroom paraprofessional. She had been working at P.S. 300 for about 3 years and was assigned a classroom that included bilingual students in order to capitalize on her native tongue of Spanish. Linda's current classroom duties included communicating with the English Language Learners' (ELL) parents, modifying the curriculum to fit the needs of the students, working in small group settings with all students, and generally assisting the teachers. Jackie and Candace tried to feed off Linda's skills. For instance, Linda used to be a seamstress of wedding dresses. During the class's center time, Linda ran a sewing center in which the children created pillows. Near the end of the year, as part of a community study for social studies, the students created individual quilt squares which became part of a class community quilt.

Linda was 50 years old and the mother of three children. Although she was perceived as another teacher in the classroom, she possessed a motherly relationship with the students. The students formed a different bond with Linda than with their teachers because she is required to spend lunch and recess with the children. This allowed her to see their different sides and as a result get to know the children on a more personal level. In April a small bumblebee doll was missing from the class's poetry box. The classroom was thoroughly searched and students were asked if they had seen the missing doll. After 2 weeks, the doll had still not turned up. Very quietly one little girl approached Linda during recess and pulled the bumblebee doll from her pocket. With tears in her eyes, she told her that she just found it in her book bag and did not know it was there. She asked Linda to tell Jackie and Candace. The child felt more comfortable approaching Linda than either Jackie or Candace. In this way, Linda served as a liaison between the children and the teachers. They confided in Linda.

Despite a limited time to meet and confer with classroom teachers, Linda still seemed to find time to always be on the same page as the teachers. She came in early in the morning and stayed late in the afternoons. She was also very involved in the school community. She worked the after-school program and attended school social events. She was even present at all parent–teacher conferences although she was only required to be available during conferences with the English Language Learners' parents.

In both schools, a paraprofessional was present to assist with the students. However, the effectiveness and role of each were clearly different, despite the similarities in their professional duties. This illustrates that common planning time and clear and constant communication between the paraprofessional and teacher are essential for creating a positive learning community for the students. In addition, a teacher's attitude and behavior toward the paraprofessional can dictate and/or foster certain (positive or negative) relationships between the teacher and the paraprofessional and between the paraprofessional and students.

Behavior Reinforcement

The language, reinforcement, and reward systems used in the two classrooms also differed. In my fifth-grade placement, the whole class was on the same reward system. Each table was assigned a letter, A through F. These letters were written on the board. Letters were first circled and then erased based on inappropriate behavior such as fighting or talking. If the letter was still on the board by the end of the day, then that table or tables would get a star on the star chart. Whatever table(s) reached the end of the star chart first, the members of that table(s) would get a reward (school stationery). If the whole class was tied and reached the end of the star chart at the same time then they got a pizza party. If the same children persisted in their negative behavior then a phone call was made to their home. The students seemed motivated by the star chart but also blamed specific children for their lack of success. When new seating arrangements were made students were vocal about which children they did not want at their tables because they knew that they were often the reason stars got removed.

It seemed to me that the star chart system did not encourage children to take responsibility for their own actions, but rather served to encourage blaming of each other, and once the letter was lost it could not be earned back. Children frequently yelled at each other for getting their stars removed which resulted in even more talking and inappropriate behavior. After I completed my student teaching semester I returned once to visit. I noticed that Fred was seated by himself next to the teacher's desk. I asked him what had happened and he answered that he was not allowed to be part of any team because he couldn't control his behavior and as a result it was unfair for the others. His own desk had his own letter for his behavior alone.

The classroom environment felt like one of hostility and competition. When one particular student was called on the rest of the class erupted into groans and moans. Children constantly sucked their teeth at the success of other children. The same three children were consistently used as the positive examples for the class. One girl, Anna, an immigrant from the Philippines who was extremely soft-spoken and quiet, always went beyond assignment guidelines and handed in magnificent pieces of work. On one occasion, the children were instructed to make time lines of their lives. Anna brought in an elaborate piece of laminated poster board with colored photographs and printed colored labels and captions. Many other children ran into the room that morning eager to exhibit their time lines. Rather than addressing everyone's successful efforts, my cooperating teacher spent approximately 10 minutes discussing why Anna was going to be successful in life. The whole time she had Anna standing up and holding up her beautiful time line. While praising Anna's work she pointed to other students' work to demonstrate their lack of effort. It is important to note that this school contains a very diverse student population. Some students come from upper to middle-class homes but quite a few others come from public housing projects in the neighborhood. Some children had no art supplies at home, not even crayons. Looking at the time lines, all the children completed the assignment accurately. They showed the progression of their life from birth until the fifth grade. Some children did this in more creative and colorful ways, perhaps due to availability of resources, adult assistance, or simple motivation. Although the children praised Anna for her work they made fun of other people's in comparison to Anna's magnificent display.

Unlike my first placement, the first-grade class did not share one behavior reinforcement plan. The class was expected to cooperate and follow classroom rules like talking in turn and working together. Classroom rules were created as a class in the beginning of the year, signed by all the students, and were clearly displayed on the classroom wall. A couple of students had more difficulty than most other children and as a result were put on their own reinforcement plans. Three children in the classroom had their own clipboards with checklists indicating their own appropriate behavior. The students received a certain number of tokens based on how many checks they had on their clipboards. They each could cash in a predetermined number of tokens for a reward decided upon by the child (such as computer or free-play time). These plans were individualized. All three were on reinforcement plans but they each were very different. The rest of the class seemed to understand that certain students had plans and others did not.

Jackie, Candace, and Linda were consistently engaged in positive talk. Children were always encouraged for what they could do, rather than reprimanded for what they couldn't do. For example, if a child who was struggling with consonant blends finally pronounced them correctly then all three teachers encouraged the child. Students in the classroom felt important. Every accomplishment, no matter how small, was celebrated in this first-grade classroom. During daily morning meeting, students were asked if they had big news to share. This allows students to share some of their personal lives with the class and thus contributes to building a strong community atmosphere. Many times during writing workshop student work was displayed on the overhead as a model for the other children. The teachers made sure to not always use the same children's work, although it is easy to do that. They looked purposefully into all the children's work and extracted meaningful examples to share with the rest of the class. Children were of course proud to have their work displayed on the overhead. After using one of Adam's poems to illustrate onomatopoeias, he asked for one week straight if his other pieces could also be displayed. He also proceeded to remind me that his piece was on the overhead on the afternoon that I was not in the classroom for writing workshop.

The students and teachers were constantly giving each other high-fives. During any classroom discussion, children were able to clap using the ASL sign (shaking both hands in the air) when they wanted to praise another child or something that was said. These first graders embraced opportunities to praise each other. Like any other classroom, however, this one had its share of punishment and reprimanding but it did not take place in the middle of the classroom. Children were taken aside and talked to. The students had a role to play in their own behavior management. They were given signals, such as certain looks and taps on the shoulder, to help them redirect their behavior. Recess time was deducted and in the worst-case scenarios students were put in the Pre-K class to show them the difference in behavior from a pre-kindergartner to a first grader.

THE END OF MY SEARCH FOR A PERFECT CLASSROOM

I had two extremely different student teaching experiences. In both, I found myself constantly taking stock and having to step back rather than step in. As a student teacher in the classroom you are a guest and are not able to do things your way. In the beginning of a student teaching placement especially, it is hard to completely understand your role in that classroom. I was constantly making sure I was not stepping on any toes. Many times I had to put my thoughts and feelings aside and do things I did not agree with such as participate in guided reading groups using worksheets from teacher's guides.

My program at Teachers College was extremely supportive and provided me with many opportunities to analyze what was happening in my classroom. Through constant dialogue with my supervisor and student teaching seminar group I was able to deal with my own feelings of guilt and lack of control; I discovered ways to make small positive impressions on the children such as pulling the one child aside in my fifth-grade classroom to talk to him about the word "retard." Also, during my lessons I tried to integrate cooperative learning and team building to increase the sense of community in both classrooms. I definitely had to be proactive in seeking this support and help but without it all I would not have been able to make it through an extremely challenging semester. In the end, however, I did walk away with a new set of lenses through which to view not only inclusion, but education in general. But do my stories paint the picture of an inclusive environment? How will I know when an environment is truly inclusive? How did those fifth- and first-grade classroom environments affect the students?

After completing these two student teaching placements, I naturally tended to compare and contrast them in order to find the answer to my question of a truly inclusive environment. I now have to wonder if there is such a thing. Although my experiences were extremely different I walked away with so much knowledge and insight from both classrooms. I entered my student teaching placements thinking they would be perfect models for

me to emulate in my own future classroom. I quickly learned that there is
no such thing as a perfect classroom. I came looking for a truly inclusive environment and I leave realizing that I understand the pieces that make inclusion successful, but I have yet to find perfection. However, I feel that I
cannot keep searching for that "perfect" classroom because it may not exist.
What may work in one classroom might not work in another and what one
teacher does in her classroom might seem crazy to me but might actually be
serving a purpose for her students. My journey in inclusive education has
taught me that I must be inclusive in my thinking. Teaching, more specifically teaching inclusively, is not a skill that some possess and some do not. It
is a craft that one must work at and build on. I now begin my teaching career with a small foundation, which includes a year of student teaching experiences, a binder full of journal entries, boxes full of papers, journal articles, and books, all dealing with inclusive education, and all containing
hopes upon which to build.

QUESTIONS

For Discussion and Reflection

- How do you think teaching assistants or paraprofessionals are best utilized in the classroom? What will you need to do as a teacher to bring
  this into existence?
- How can teachers attend to students' different needs without segregating them academically or socially from the peer group?
- What ways can teachers work with limited time schedules for coplan-
  ning lessons and activities? How does this spirit of cooperation between teachers affect students' learning in the classroom?

In the Field

- Listen and keep track of educators' public comments about students.
  Analyze what you think the purpose might be of their comments. Discuss how the students reacted to different types of comments. What
  can you take from this analysis for your own teaching?
- What are the models of collaboration between special education and
  general education (e.g., coteaching between general and special educators; part-time consulting teacher) in your school? In your district?
  In your state? Try to observe at least two different models. What do you

think is most important for teachers to know and be able to do within each of the models you have observed?

- Interview a number of paraprofessionals or teaching assistants and find out from them what they think the most important aspects of their jobs are. Ask them what they think is most important for teachers to know about working well with teaching assistants.

Chapter 3

Barbara Wang's Inquiry: How Teachers Foster Peer Relationships

> *Life in schools is characterized by human communication—the language (silent and spoken) that permeates the environment and affects relationships, interactions, efforts, and outcomes.*
>
> —Beatrice Fennimore, *Talk Matters* (2000, p. 111)

As student teachers, we are given the precarious role of observing classroom situations from the outside, while not truly being an outsider. Unlike most other observers, we are also given the opportunity to see the same classroom over and over again. We see the good days and the bad days. We witness moments of awe that catch our eye like the sparkly glint of something on a sunny sidewalk, when for a split second we ask ourselves, "What *is* that?" We teeter on being neutral sponges of knowledge and critical, infiltrating judges. We have the opportunity to see what it is that even the teachers themselves do not or cannot see. Children are extremely perceptive when it comes to how teachers treat certain students: It's often blatantly obvious who the favorites are, who the troublemakers are, and which ones the teachers just can't stand. Over the course of our placement, student teachers begin to see the children for who they are, every situation for what it symbolizes, and the peer exchanges that they generate. The way students understand teacher's preferential treatment can manifest itself into who will sit next to whom at lunch, who will receive a "Good morning" salutation and often, who will become friends with whom. In this chapter, I explore the question of the teacher's role in helping to develop peer interactions and how a teacher's own behavior and attitudes toward particular students can influence this development.

MY INQUIRY INTO SOCIAL RELATIONSHIPS

In chapter 2, Carine's story of her cooperating teacher at P.S. 700 reflects, somewhat, things that I have also seen in my student teaching placements and elsewhere. What I have come to question and continue to question, is the role that teachers play in fostering peer relationships and the construction of the classroom community. How can teachers become aware of their own biased behaviors so that they do not cause irreparable damage to this community? Like Jen (chapter 6), I also came to find discrepancies between theory and practice. So while some teachers were adamant about creating cohesive classrooms through cooperation and heterogeneous groupings, what they said and how they reacted to certain students could be seen as counteracting their stated objectives. This chapter narratively chronicles my experiences in inclusive classrooms, both during and prior to student teaching with the essential component focusing on questions; these questions arose not necessarily from a specific university assignment, but rather out of frustration. They are questions that I wanted answers to, but knew not to expect would be fully answered. As Celia described in her introduction, when the Inclusion Study Group initially met, we talked. We complained. We asked questions. We voiced our concerns. And at that time I was concerned by what seemed like an alarming trend in my classroom experiences. What unfolded, was this chapter. In writing this chapter, I have come up with even more questions, more concerns, and deeper insights than I had when I first began writing. Allowing myself to rethink, analyze, and sometimes scrutinize my past experiences and actions has unveiled a gamut of new thoughts to teaching inclusively.

It is often said that we teach who we are. If this is the case, then who are we? Yet, more specifically, who am I? As a future teacher, I think the struggle lies between the questions, "Do we teach who we are? Do we teach that with which we are the most familiar and comfortable with? Do we teach who we *want* to become?" As our conception of who we are as individuals and as teachers constantly changes, we begin to mesh our new ideas and experiences with those of the past. These past experiences are often inescapable, regardless of how often we try to avoid or suppress them. They have shaped who we are and in some cases, who we *do not* want to become. Consciously or unconsciously, how, and in what environment we were raised affects who we are today. And as teachers, this translates into the way we teach and respond to children.

As I have spent more and more time in classrooms, I have noticed how vital the teacher is in creating the classroom environment: classrooms that either exude cooperation and cohesion or those that exemplify competition and ostracization. I feel that this role becomes even more essential in light of inclusive classrooms and in light of our society that continues to capitalize on segregative practices. How our students and their parents view people with disabilities (people who will one day become their coworkers, peers, neighbors, and friends) depends on their early experiences and interactions—experiences and interactions that are often framed by us, the classroom teachers. I question, how does one, like me, with little experience in inclusive classrooms overcome her "environments" to provide this essential social framework? How can we become aware of our biases so that they do not interfere with our classroom community?

WORKING AS A TEACHING ASSISTANT

"Sunday, Monday, Tuesday, Wednesday . . ." chorused through my head, tag teaming from the left side to the right. I was staring blankly at the two classes, although I think I was still smiling. Mrs. Norton and Mrs. Evans were singing simultaneously, though not together, creating a round-like effect. The children sat attentively, side by side in groups in front of their teachers, mesmerized by the performances. The boy in the overalls was swaying side to side, his size making him instantly recognizable and distinct. The girl with the bunny was still crying. This is how every morning would begin: with both the singing and the crying. It wasn't until December when the crying would finally end. And it wasn't until much later when I recognized the impact that these kindergarten classes had had on me, both personally and professionally.

Encountering Students With Significant Needs

Thus began my journey back into the "educational compound." The place where I felt safe and comfortable. Where things were familiar and simple. But as I soon came to realize, these things just were not so. I had just finished college with no aspirations of returning to school—unless it was grad school, and I definitely did not have elementary school in mind. I accepted the job as an "educational aide" thinking to myself, "How difficult could it actually be?" I figured going back to elementary school would be like riding a bike—something that you'd never forget regardless of how long it has been since you actually rode one. It was just a matter of practice, being re-exposed to the "bike."

Well, unlike riding a bike, this was different. It had absolutely nothing to do with re-exposure. I, after all, was not a student who suddenly found myself back in school. I was an *adult* this time around. I had responsibilities. I was a role model. *What?!* I was the youngest sibling. Everyone was always taking care of *me*. Helping *me*. Telling *me* what to do. How could I possibly assist anyone, let alone two teachers and four classes of 107 kindergarteners?

What was I thinking? What was the principal thinking in hiring me? And what did she mean by saying "children with special needs"? A week into the job and I was still worried that I had taken on too much.

Though I hate using the proverbial "things were different when I was a kid" saying (it makes me feel old), but things were. My exposure to children with special needs, actually any person with special needs, was severely limited, as was my understanding of their specific needs. I grew up in a system with self-contained special education classes and those were filled with students labeled with learning disabilities. I certainly didn't remember kids crawling under tables, or fleeing from classrooms, threatening to run away—labeled or not. In my elementary experience we feared the principal and listened dutifully to our teachers. We were a community identified by only our classroom number—not by similarities or differences, or cooperation. Our classrooms thrived on competition.

So to say I was shocked when kids *did* crawl under tables and sprint from the class at my brand new job would be an understatement. Saying that I felt unprepared for these situations would likewise be an understatement. I was dumbfounded. I panicked. I had relatively little experience with children and no behavioral and/or classroom management skills whatsoever. In addition to students with behavioral and emotional needs, there were many students with physical needs. Children were facing health-related issues from diseases I had never even heard about. What were the protocols that came with that? All I had were coworkers and instinct, which truthfully did not fare all that well sometimes. But, I learned a lot from observing, asking questions, and talking to other staff members. Unfortunately, most of the staff worked at the school long before it became inclusive; many teachers were hesitant about the incentives of inclusion, some were downright resentful. Most, however, just felt unprepared to teach to the diverse population of children that now inhabited the school. Myself included.

The 2 years that I spent at that school encompassed a hands-on, crash course in special education and inclusion. I was exposed to some of the vocabulary, specialists, and procedures. I was overwhelmed by feelings: bombarded by frustration and guilt. I was placed in a role that required ubiquity and flexibility, one that I found to be extremely difficult. I constantly felt torn between what the teachers needed, what individual children needed and the needs of the "rest" of the class. I was frustrated that I couldn't do everything or help everyone. Reiterating my lack of experience with children in general and diverse environments, I constantly found myself distinguishing between "those" kids and "everyone" else. I don't know why. Perhaps it was because the teachers did. Maybe it was because the children did so as well. When I prioritized my time that's how the breakdown was—children with special needs and children without. And at the time, I did make that distinguishing factor, I did so without much thought or hesitation. I have to admit that I did many things early on without thinking. It wasn't until much later that I could recognize or even consider alternative reasons for my categorization.

NARRATIVE ONE: THE CASE OF THOMAS

It was a beautiful afternoon, surprisingly hot, especially for the end of September. Mrs. Norton and Mrs. Evans felt that it was a necessity for children to be able to go outside and play—to run around wildly with reckless (but safe) abandon. They often took this time to plan for the next day or to get things ready to send home while I accompanied the classes outside. Today was like any ordinary day outside; I was watching the children chase each other around and around the playground. I always got nervous when they ran too close to the swing set, afraid that one unaware victim would get kicked in the head. As with most nice days, there were groups of children playing different games—Tag, Duck-Duck-Goose . . . while others romped on the equipment.

Twenty minutes. Twenty minutes ticking away methodically like drops from a leaking faucet. Twenty minutes always seemed like such a long time, but today it seemed like an eternity. It was probably the heat from the midday sun, or the never-ending tattling. It was a day of tattling. James was under the slide throwing sand and Sara wouldn't let others across the monkey bars. One after another, they came. They came with stories of wrongdoing and delinquency. It was days like this that made time pass slowly. Ever so slowly. And just when I thought that time couldn't pass any slower, they came. Gradually I could hear the rumblings from afar. They became louder and louder, until there was that beautiful sound. That *glorious* sound. The sound that fell somewhere between a squeal and a squawk: quick and to the point. The bus drivers were putting the big yellow buses into park. One by one, they pulled into the drive, their salutations echoing across the playground. Even though they were parking on the other side of the school, I knew that #25 was there waiting and #34 was in as well. They were always, and I mean always, the first two buses in. Yes! It was *finally* time to go home.

I called the classes to go in, kids scrambling from every which way, a stampede in progress. They knew instinctively where to go, Mrs. Evans' class on the left, Mrs. Norton's on the right. They knew how to stand, in a single-file line, one behind another. They all came. That is, they all came, except one. Over by the climbing equipment, Thomas was under the slide, playing in the sand. "C'mon, let's go, Thomas. It's time to line up. The buses are here," I called. No reaction. Taking a few steps closer, I said again, "Let's go. We have to go in." "Nope, I'm not going." Thomas was now standing with his arms crossed firmly over his chest. He had his head stuck up into the air and turned away from the group. This was a gesture that he often did when he was either trying to ignore people or show his displeasure. Another gimmick was putting his hands over his ears and "La-la-la-ing" until things were over. Time was ticking. Precious time. Time that initially crawled all day was now racing by. The first load of buses was going to leave in 10 minutes. There were still papers to hand out, book bags to pack, and chairs to put up. And with 5-year-olds, this took *time.*

"Ahhh—hurry up!" I wanted to scream, but instead out came, "Thomas, the buses are here. We need to go," the desperation in my voice still undetectable. Thomas, still in his stance, yelled, "I'm *not* going home." AHHHH! Maybe if I went over to talk to him, I could reason with him. Find out what was going on. Convince him to line up. But, there was no time, "*THOMAS,*" I pleaded. Still nothing. Okay. So the plan was to go over there and retrieve him. Hold his hand and lead him in. Simple enough. As I took the first few steps, Thomas dashed out from behind the slide and took off toward the far end of the yard—the part of the yard that bordered the parking lot of a church on one side and a busy road on the other. He looked around, left to right, planning an escape route. If he even goes into the lot . . . and then, he stopped.

He stood perfectly still, staring and flashing a wide, toothy grin. There he stood, taunting me, I thought. I took two steps forward. He took off to the left toward the woods—well at least it was away from the road—and stopped. AHHHH—he thinks it's a game! So even if I did give chase, what would I do if I caught him? Tackle him? Sit on him? Sling him over my shoulder and carry him in? And, what about everyone else? Should I just leave them there? With my head reeling in debate, I opted for, "Thomas, get in line right now or else you won't be having recess tomorrow!" I yelled. The infamous, "Do this, or else" statement. To counter my feelings of having no control of situations, I depended on these statements a lot. Meanwhile both classes, still in single-file lines, watched.

Stricken with anger, annoyance, and fear (what happens if he did run away?), I panicked and said, "We're going in now, Thomas, and *I'm* going to get *Mrs. Evans.*" Hoping to scare him, the threat did not work. As I have since learned threats do not work well with children or in classrooms. They usually end up backfiring, creating more chaos and anxiety. Knowing that we were already late for the buses, I bolted back to the lines, led them in backwards, all the while staring at Thomas hovering by the edge of the yard. He did not run after us (as I had hoped) and did not even move. As we entered the building, the children were already badgering Mrs. Evans with, "Thomas is still outside! He wouldn't line up. He ran away!" as I fought to explain the situation calmly. I pointed out the window to Thomas, who was still standing along the tree line of the yard. She told me to go get the principal and she dashed out the door.

Luckily, Mrs. Norton held down the fort while we prepared for battle. I returned to the scene, armed with the principal. Mrs. Evans was in the room already, but Thomas was not. She said that when he saw her coming out of the building, he took off toward the parking lot again. She called to him and told him to get on the bus. Still nothing. "Well, I guess we'll have to call his mother to come pick him up," sighed the principal. She shrugged her shoulders, shook her head, and marched out into the blinding sunlight.

Unfortunately many days ended with Thomas's mother picking him up. Actually, Thomas very rarely made it to the end of the day—even though classes were only 2½ hours long. With every infraction—crawling under tables, running around the hallways—he missed recess, lost center time, went to the principal's office. In severe cases, he was sent home. I accompanied Thomas to the principal's office. I took way too many trips to the principal's office, shuttling him to and fro, and it was something that I despised. Oftentimes, I was expected to give an explanation or account of the infraction when many times, I didn't know. Most of the time, I either said, "He was having a difficult day," or "Mrs. Evans asked me to bring him here. I don't know what happened." Every time though, I felt as if I were the one at fault, the one being judged. The one who couldn't "handle" the situation. I felt myself wanting to place blame on someone, anyone—myself, the teachers, the principal and unfortunately the children.

As for the differentiation between "those" kids and the rest of the class, maybe I needed some kind of reassurance that *I* was not "at fault." That their behavior was on account of something innate within them—something beyond my control. That I could only do so much, before things were out of my hands. I imagine that more than likely, perhaps I was projecting my feeling of frustration and annoyance onto "those" children because of the increasing isolation I began to feel in the classroom. Mrs. Norton and Mrs. Evans became progressively more dependent on me to handle difficult children or remove them from the classroom because they were a distraction to the "rest" of the class. In essence, it was easier for *them*, the teachers, to have particular children out of the room but meanwhile, it was less time that I had to spend with the "others." When particular children were not in the room, it almost seemed like a different class. The children seemed calmer. They appeared to pay closer attention to the seemingly more jovial teachers. There was less yelling and way less reprimanding. It seemed easier for everyone—everyone except Thomas.

Thomas had previously attended the district's prekindergarten program as did many of the other children in the class. He did not, however, have the friendships and relationships that the others had. None of the children acknowledged his presence on the first day of school, as they did the others who were also in Pre-K. And the more he was yelled at and the more he ran off (while we gave chase), the more the children distanced themselves from him. It started off with subtle shifts on the carpet when he went to sit down. A little to the left or a little to the right. Then, children stood up and moved to different places when he arrived. Finally, children would say to him, point blank, "Don't sit next to me." Through all of this, there was no attempt to make him a part of the class. Indeed, with all of his removals, he was truly being excluded and the community mirrored this. Would things have been different if the teachers treated him differently than they had? Would it have made any difference if we had made any attempts to make him *be* a member of the community?

With each of the consequences that Thomas faced—no recess, going home—we were looking to change his behavior, to alter him in some way. We were looking to make Thomas "fit into" the class. But now I question, what changes could have been made to his environment? Maybe he *needed* shorter days or fewer days of school. Maybe he needed fewer children in the classroom and more adult supports. Maybe he needed many more things that were not provided in the classroom or even in the school. Of course all of these insights came in hindsight, but, still, for all of the other Thomases out there, how do you figure out what those things are? How do you provide support and assistance for all of the children, with or without special needs, when there is only *one* of you? What I realize now, is the lack of support—both professional and emotional—for staff members at this school. There seemed to be few resources available to teachers like educational materials on teaching in inclusive classrooms and to diverse populations. There also were very few people to assist in the classroom. Although arguments can also be made against having too many people in the class, I think that some assistance is necessary and could dispel a lot of frustration and anxiety for teachers. And I don't mean assistance in removing children.

CAN I TEACH STUDENTS WITH COMPLEX EMOTIONAL NEEDS?

I walked away from this school intrigued by teaching and inclusion. I wanted to pursue the "technical" aspects of teaching. I wanted to do lessons and read stories—answer questions and help to propagate them. I wanted to explore new ideas and concepts with students because I feel that I have just as much to learn from them as they do from me. I had discovered the intrinsically fascinating world of children, their thinking and learning. To be able to see the look on their faces when they had an "Aha!" moment was both exhilarating and gratifying. And yet, having been introduced to the confusing realm of inclusion—the terminology, the pitfalls, the successes— I was also scared about teaching. There was obviously much more to teaching than I had expected. I had so many questions and concerns. A part of me felt that learning and knowing more about inclusion and inclusive practices would make me a better teacher regardless of where I ended up working. I also believed that social change comes through education and thus, inclusive schools. Promoting inclusion would be the first steps in combating society's segregative practices. But, the other part felt that if this was what inclusion entailed, I'd be better off running the other way. Internal struggle aside, I remained committed to learning more about inclusion. Even not having any prior experiences in teaching, I could see that there was nothing inclusive about this particular school's practices. There was nothing inclusive about exclusion. There was nothing inclusive about having a high-management child sitting in the hallway day after day because the teacher didn't know what else to do. I left wondering, so if this wasn't inclusion, what was? What did it look like? How could it be done *well*? What was inclusion's place in other school systems? What would inclusion's place be in my classroom?

"We All Have Special Needs . . ."

As I wandered further down the road through the educational compound, I found myself at the door of a progressive, alternative school in the city. "It will be a perfect place to work while I pursue my teaching degree," I thought to myself. It was indeed. Well, sort of. Through the course of a year, I ventured where I had never been before. I underwent intense scrutiny from both myself and others. I learned more about myself this year than in all my years combined. Nothing could have prepared me for this experience. It was mentally and physically difficult to go to work everyday, just completely exhausting.

Still wanting to pursue greater insights into inclusion, I asked the principal whether or not the school served children with special needs. "We all have special needs," was the reply, and in short, that is precisely what I would experience in that year. I found myself in position where exceptions were the norm, everyone had an individualized education plan, though they were not technically nor officially IEPs. Some were, most were not. "Appropriate" conduct was not in the school repertoire. The staff did not have the training or resources for the population of children that attended the school: Students and teacher were hit and kicked repeatedly on a daily basis by certain students. The administration, on the other hand, would blame the teachers and say that they were not working with the students in the "right way," although no way was ever specifically stated. Concerns were dismissed and requests for help were ignored. When help was asked for in working with a well-known difficult-to-manage child, the principal responded with, "If anyone knew what to do, we wouldn't be here," and walked away. I learned to doubt myself whenever any decision had to be made. I doubted my abilities and capabilities. I was basically miserable, as were many others, both teachers and students alike. It was just not a place where I wanted to be. It made me question whether or not I really wanted to teach—EVER!

From this experience, I have learned that even in light of the most difficult circumstances and experiences, new knowledge and appreciation is gained. I did learn a lot from this experience—more so about myself than anything else, but most importantly as a teacher, of the importance of a support network. The school system is not a place where you want to be working alone. I think that even though teachers are crusaders for children, they also need to be crusaders for each other. The network must also be made up of administrators. If they are not going to support you and have confidence in your abilities and decisions, I have to wonder now, who will? Teaching is also about learning, and learning often requires asking for, no, *demanding*, help.

This experience also helped me in realizing that schools are emotional places. They are filled with excitement, fear, anger, and apathy—felt by everyone: teachers, students, parents, and staff. The most difficult thing for me was coming to terms with my own emotions. How children's words and actions were hurtful to me, or that sometimes they made me angry. Children can induce so many feelings, especially the negative ones. My own "aha" moment came a year later, when I recognized that I could be angry or annoyed at children, possibly even (gasp!) dislike some of them, but that I didn't have to act on my feelings. I didn't need to yell or scream when *I* was mad. I didn't have to bring them treats or bribes so they'd like me. I didn't have to even like ALL of them. Being able to recognize my feelings and not act or react upon them, has been the most beneficial to my student teaching experiences. After all, we all have special needs . . .

OBSERVING THE SOCIAL CLIMATE IN MY STUDENT TEACHING PLACEMENTS

It was after these experiences with inclusion that I started my year of student teaching. Still wanting and needing to see inclusion done well—what was *well*, I honestly don't know, I asked to be part of the Inclusion Study Group. As such, I was placed in two collaborative team teaching classrooms, the first semester in kindergarten and the second, in fifth grade. Equipped with enhanced ideologies and a stronger sense of self, I still couldn't help but be fearful of what I would (or wouldn't) encounter. Though I had recognized that I didn't have to like all of my students, I still did have to teach *all* of them. How I could accomplish this, launched the next leg of my journey.

In Theory . . .

From the onset, teachers try to prevent exclusion by creating a cooperative, caring environment through the everyday curriculum. At least, that's what some say. In speaking to various K–2 teachers at my placements, they felt that the greatest strategy to increase social structures—developing the will to work together—is accomplished through various center activities. Two of their favorite center times for this are dramatic play and block building. During these activities, all children have a role. Not necessarily an equal role (in a true cooperative sense) but a role that is an important contributing factor to the entire piece, activity, or building. Everyone has an active role. Without each piece, the building lies incomplete.

Along with the actual block-building skills needed, a lot of socialization skills are also necessary. What kinds of words would be needed to ask for blocks? How about to share a new idea or negotiate a new structure? What would happen if something accidentally fell? What happens if you were the one to knock it over? In addition to being a time for learning from these specific activities, it is also a time for teachers to continue to model positive behaviors, and to acknowledge when they see positive behaviors. Having the ability to consider suggestions from classmates and alternative sources begins to pave the way for future collaborative efforts with classmates: In order to have the will to work together children need to be able to listen to each other. The idea of teaching social skills is also supported by others in the field of instruction. By teaching these skills to the whole class—skills that encourage in essence the values of cooperation, politeness, honesty—teachers can encourage the development of peer relationships between students with disabilities and students without (Snell & Janney, 2000).

The same K–2 teachers also believed that teaching communication skills is (ideally) an ongoing process in the classroom, something most easily done through positive modeling. The teachers suggested modeling kind and appropriate ways of asking for materials, for example. Others said modeling could be used to show possible conversations children could have with their walking partner. A kindergarten teacher said that she realized that not all of her students come from homes where basic communication skills are taught or reinforced. Some children don't know "how to ask for things," but need to be shown how. Others need to be shown how to participate in a conversation; how to listen carefully, ask questions, or respond to what someone else has said.

Many of the primary teachers believed in choosing walking partners for the children. This, they said, helped to foster relationships between children who might never have chosen each other as partners. They are given the opportunity to notice things together, help each other, and share experiences/stories with one another. Especially at the beginning of the year, many felt that this is an effective way in allowing all of the children to get to know one another, and to avoid the cliquish groups that can form. Being familiar with everyone in the class also leads into developing the social skills structures within the classroom. Fostering the development of communication skills is one of the most basic skills in these grades. It is a time when children are taught and then constantly reminded, to use their words instead of their bodies (as in hitting or grabbing) to express themselves.

The teacher's role in facilitating friendships has been at the center of much research. Hamre-Nietupski and Hendrickson (1994) conducted a survey of 312 K–12, general education teachers in Nebraska, Iowa, and Florida on their perceptions on facilitating friendships between students with severe disabilities and their nondisabled peers. The results suggested that the educators believed both special education and general education teachers were primarily responsible for facilitating friendships. One of the questions that the survey asked was, "What strategies can adults use to help facilitate these friendships?" The survey listed several choices, which in turn, the educators ranked. The top five choices for general education teachers were: implementing cooperative learning approaches that emphasize children learning together; collaborate with special education teachers; teach social interaction skills to students with and without disabilities; teach nondisabled students to be peer tutors and/or partners; and present information on disabilities to children, staff, and parents. The lowest ranked strategies included: encourage parents to create interaction opportunities outside school; modify curriculum/instructional strategies to promote friendship building; and seek additional training—in-service or university (p. 111). So, some teachers seem to be in agreement that adults, especially teachers, are in the position to facilitate friendships between students with and without disabilities, but what happens when in addition to these essential communication and social skills they unwittingly model their own biases? What happens when they allow their annoyance and frustration for one child (or several) to permeate their community? How do we teach "tolerance" when we, ourselves, do not exhibit it?

The Case of Steven

It began the first day of school. "Steven, stop running." "Steven, go wash your hands." "Steven, don't push." "Steven, *STOP IT*." It seemed never ending. In the hallways, in the park, in the classroom. It almost always came from the teachers. Then, it came from the students. Almost inevitably, Steven replied, "Okay," and he stopped. Also, inevitably, it would happen again. He would push. He would grab. He would sneeze without covering his mouth. And like clockwork, "*Steven. . . .*" Unlike regular beginning of the year routines that get hammered out with time and practice, Steven just

never seemed to "get" it. Regardless of the number of times he was told, or
yelled at, Steven never complied. This of course led to great frustration for
the teachers, the students, and even some parents. One parent went so far
as to tell her son that Steven was "so bad he was going to be sent to the bad
boys' school."

In *Talk Matters* (2000), Fennimore asks us to reshape the language used
in public schools; the dialogue among educators, staff, parents, and visitors,
as well as the descriptors used to label the progress of children need to be
extremely well thought out. She has pointed out that the power which negative educational language has is not just in what kind of public opinion is
created regarding American children, but that the language "actually
shapes the school experiences and educational outcomes of students" (p.
4). Therefore, when plagued by negative labels and opinions, children often experience school negatively. I wonder, is this how children in this classroom are experiencing school? Is it just the beginning of a long line of what
some children will see as "bad" school experiences? If children in this classroom were being affected by negative language, educational or not, how
would we know? Being in the precarious role of student teacher, I observed,
I analyzed.

As the semester wore on, I began to notice shifts in the community. I noticed that gentle reminders became stern commands: Voices were louder
and stronger when addressing Steven. Steven received a smaller number of
positive reinforcements or praises (if any) than the other students. During
Choice Time, fewer and fewer children elected to go to the block center
when Steven was there, even though it was usually an extremely popular
center. I noticed that Steven always played in the park by himself. I also noticed that Steven was not the only student being excluded. In this classroom, Steven was not the only student singled out. The teachers had painfully excluded certain children during pairing up for partners (when
walking to specials, lunch, or the park) so that either one of two things happened: The excluded ones were called last so that they would walk with
each other or with a teacher; or when the children got to choose their own
partners, the "others" would refuse to walk with them and they would be
left to walk with each other or a teacher. These "certain" children were almost always the children with disabilities. Seeing the same scenario day after day, and the looks on both the rejected child and the child doing the re-
jecting, became a painful sight for me. How can one pretend to not see the
pattern, or the disappointment? How can one not notice when the same
child is left sitting on the rug with no partner? Many would tend to believe,
or want to believe, that the child does not notice the rejection: that they are
too "out of it" to know. However, I knew. Steven knew. He even came to expect me to be his "partner" every day—going to the end of the line, waiting,
arm outstretched. For Steven, this was the one thing he did get.

I constantly wondered, "Why was it that Steven was always called to get in line last?" Why was it that he was almost always paired with another student with special needs or a teacher? Why was it that no one wanted to play with him, or walk with him, or sit next to him? What I realize is that I had been pursuing a line of questioning that I had no chance of answering. It wasn't necessarily "*Why* this or *why* that." What I should have been asking is *how*. How could I have helped the other children want to be with Steven? How could the routines be structured so that no one was singled out? How could the theory actually be put into practice?

In time, it seemed as though the community was disjointed. It seemed like a community at times, and then not so at others. The teachers had spent a great deal of time focusing on differences and similarities in the classroom, which was a benefit to all of the students. The children did learn respect and tolerance and cooperation and models of helping, but there seemed to still be a difference in socialization. During times of free play or center time, the children with special needs were still excluded. Many times, they played together by themselves. How can we facilitate a community that goes beyond the academics and the classroom walls? How can we promote peer relationships that extend into actual friendships and not just "interactions"?

When Is Peer Support Patronizing?

In addition to Steven, Sophie was another student who was consistently excluded, in part because she was often segregated with her assistant. Sophie had Down syndrome and had relatively limited oral communication skills. She sought out her assistant constantly and had few interactions with the other children. Her assistant sat next to her on the rug. Her assistant helped her in class, during lunch, and at the park. Where Sophie was, her assistant was sure to be found and not a single classmate around. With support from her parents, the teachers, and other adults, Sophie was encouraged to play with other classmates and they were encouraged to play with Sophie (or help her when needed).

As the semester progressed, I observed that the nature of Sophie's relationship with her classmates began to change. The children played with Sophie, they hugged her. They helped her with the "little" things like zipping up her coat or walking down the stairs. The class was finally engaged with Sophie! However, the teachers were upset. They were annoyed. The thing that bothered them was that during various types of play, Sophie was always designated as the "baby" or was treated like a baby. Unfortunately, from my observations, that is exactly how the teachers (and other adults in the classroom) treated her. Every time the teachers addressed Sophie, the tone of their voices would take on a high-pitched, baby-talk voice and they would only use short two- or three-word commands or appraisals. As Fenni-more (2000) reminds us, "the language environment also is determined by *every adult who works and interacts with the children*" (p. 111). The adults also used many more touch tactics with her than with the other students, things such as a pat on the head, a stroke on the cheek. Maybe some part of the children's play reflected the nurturing, helping role that many of the students (particularly the girls) took on, but I also think that the teachers' behaviors and tendencies toward Sophie had a direct impact on the other students and their behaviors. Not only was the language environment in the classroom shaped by the teachers, but the behavioral environment was shaped by them as well. The children seemed to be imitating what they were seeing.

So although the teachers tried to discourage the "baby" role that Sophie played with the other students, they did little to modify their own behaviors. What kinds of modifications are to be done when people are (seemingly) unaware of their behaviors and the influence that they have? How can teachers develop greater self-awareness without becoming self-conscious?

By the close of my first semester of student teaching, I felt enlightened. I felt defeated. I still struggled with making inclusion "work." I was immediately reminded of my first struggles with ubiquity. How could I possibly do everything at once? How can I attend to *everyone's* needs? I was constantly making mental notes to myself—do this, restate that, check on _____; stop doing that, you forgot to do _____, you just did it again! AHHH! I probably had more conversations with myself than with other people.

**MY SECOND PLACEMENT: POCKETS OF EXCLUSION
REMAIN**

The second semester brought a whole new class, a whole new set of experiences and of course, more questions. By now, constant questions and reflections had become the norm. I finally became comfortable with the concept that not all questions had answers (both mine and my students') but, Britt, my supervisor for the semester, added a whole new dimension. What do you do when your questions are confronted by yet, more questions? Is it a confusing mess? Are you stuck in a state of perpetual reflection? What happens when you forget what it is that you are truly reflecting *about*? Do you just pretend that you're reflecting? With every one question that I had, Britt somehow offered another five. Though for some, this may seem like an annoyance, I think that this somehow increased my level of awareness—on both personal and professional levels. She made me think and rethink what I was doing in the classroom and more importantly *why* I was doing it. She gave me a glimpse of my teaching through her lenses (see chapter 7) of what was being done and what *could* be done. She saw the potential in what I could not see.

The second semester, the commute was further, the children were bigger, the material more challenging, but, the questions remained. The ones I adamantly pursued in this part of my journey were still, "How can inclusion be done well?" and "How do teachers facilitate (or impede) peer relationships?" The class was amazingly cohesive and collaborative. They worked with each other and they helped one another. For the most part, it seemed like the perfect inclusive classroom. Perhaps I had finally found it! Inclusion done well! But just as in my last placement as a student teacher, I had to, just had to, observe, analyze, and critique. I teetered from side to side, trying to find the delicate balance, the perfect fulcrum.

The Case of Catherine and John

And just when I thought that I had found it, when I was about to erupt into thunderous applause after the first act, I noticed out of the corner of my eye, two somewhat misplaced actors. They seemed awkward, out of place, constantly doing their own thing. They stood in the wings, almost contentedly. They performed not with the group, but most often by themselves or with "their" paraprofessional. Though I had come to anticipate differences in an inclusive classroom (students at different places and working at different paces), these actors not only performed by themselves academically, they also did so socially.

When I arrived in late January, Catherine and John were consistently off doing their "own thing." Whether it was working one-on-one with a paraprofessional or using computer tutorial programs, they were academically and instructionally excluded in many subject areas. With the structure of the curriculum focused on cooperative learning and group work, Catherine's and John's constant instructional isolation created fewer opportunities for social interactions with their peers—inside the classroom and I believe, unintentionally, outside of the classroom. Though Catherine and John weren't necessarily "excluded" completely from *all* social interactions or group activities, they were on the outskirts. Outskirts that I noticed manifested itself physically: They sat on the perimeters (or often off) of the rug for meetings, they sat one or two seats away from people at lunch, they always followed a few footsteps behind other people. They also rarely initiated interactions or conversations with others.

What separated Catherine and John from each other were the kinds of interactions they had with other adults and students. For whatever reasons, the ones that people had with Catherine were lighthearted, gentle, often nurturing, whereas the interactions with John were brief, stern, and often reprimanding. Though some personality characteristics may have influenced these differences in interactions, I also believe that, as was the case with Steven and Sophie, the adult interactions influenced how Catherine and John were perceived, and in turn treated by their classmates: When the teachers laughed at Catherine's actions, they laughed. When the teachers scolded John, so did the students. No one really appeared to notice the impact of these seemingly inconsequential actions.

As the heavy air about the room lifted and the collective sighs were exhaled, the classroom shifted into a chaotic frenzy. Math, the oh-so-dreaded math, was finally over and it was time for lunch. Their excruciating pain and boredom sought refuge in noise. Chairs were squawking, mouths were chattering: rustles and bangs and the occasional thud. Bodies were all over the place. As they formed themselves into the semblance of a line, a single, raised hand emerged from the pack. The hand belonged to Brian, quiet, yet sophisticatedly savvy. He says that John keeps stepping on his toes. Looking at John, who was now standing two steps behind him and looking around the room, I proclaimed loud enough for John to hear, "Have you asked John to stop stepping on your toes?" "Yes," said Brian. Mentally assessing what my next action should be, out came the question, "Do you like it when John steps on your toes?" "Not really." Where is this conversation going, I ask myself—uh, of course he doesn't like someone stepping on his toes. Who does? Turning to John, I restate the conversation: "John. Brian has asked you to stop stepping on his toes. He doesn't like it. If you have something to tell him, it's probably best to use your words. Okay?" "Okay." And off they went, John, a few footsteps behind. So perhaps that may not have been the best solution to this situation, but having witnessed how other adults react to John and remembering Steven and Thomas, maybe I could try something different. I didn't want to join the annals of yellers and snappers. Having become more increasingly aware of myself and my actions, I chose to approach John in another manner. Whether or not this made any difference was another matter entirely.

Same time, next day, same chaos. Same hand. Once again, the single hand was patiently raised in line with John not too far behind. I, however, was standing on the other side of the room when I heard, loudly, "But John, you can't do that. You can't just step on Brian's feet like that. Do you understand? *Do you understand?*" Having missed the conversation between Brian, John and my cooperating teacher, I was later informed that when asked why he was stepping on Brian, John said because he "wanted some attention." My teachers said they were amazed that John was able to verbalize this. He was "more aware" of "what was going on" than they gave him credit for. But did this change how they acted or reacted to him? Did knowing that John wanted (and needed) attention change his role or participation in class? Were there attempts to help him become a valued, participating, equal member of the class—something that has been shown to promote prosocial relationships (Salisbury & Palombaro, 1998)?

John was obviously not content standing in the wings alone as a solitary actor. I think his comment and actions far surpassed just showing his "awareness." They put into perspective the social climate of classrooms: Although some children outwardly seek attention and are consistently given it (by teachers and other students), it doesn't necessarily mean that other, less vocal students do not crave attention as well. It is our duty as teachers to *build* classroom communities; to build a social infrastructure that depends both on teacher–student and student–student interactions: meaningful interactions that reach beyond just the physical inclusion of students with disabilities.

MY COMMITMENT TO CLASSROOM BRIDGE BUILDING

In each of our chapters, we have alluded to our experiences in student teaching and teaching as "journeys." I have come to see teaching as a journey that does not necessarily have to have a particular destination in mind. It is a journey that allows one to stop at any given moment—to rest, to revitalize, to soak up the beauty of the surroundings. Each stop in the journey is not comparable; they are each special in their own way, having a different purpose and quality. Yes, there may be potholes and treacherous weather—or even some stops that may not be worth taking a picture of, but they are all still part of the journey. I have also found that occasionally, unexpected discoveries are also made. I had initially set out on my journey with one, specific destination in mind—to find inclusion done "well." Now, looking back at how far I've come, I am instead confronted with the question (surprised?), "What does 'well' actually mean?" After all, the word *well*, in and of itself, is completely subjective. And what I recognize now, is that what is well in one situation may not be well in another. What is well for me may not be for someone else. And most importantly, what is well for one class, one set of students, may not be the case for another.

In coming to this "ah-ha," I have also stumbled upon the need for teachers, for myself, to be self-aware of our behaviors and attitudes toward students in the classroom. *All* students. We have to make the commitment to reflect on our teaching. With that, we are also making the commitment to reflect on ourselves as people: who we are, who we think we are, what we believe and think we believe. As teachers, we are models for our students. And individually, we need to decide what kind of model we want to be. How can we teach inclusively and promote inclusion, when we do not model it?

As I embark upon the next leg of my journey, one that will be forever branded as "My First Year of Teaching," I still contemplate *how* I will teach. Will I teach who I am or who I want to become? What about simply teaching what is the most comfortable? A comfortability that may ignore controversial issues, avoid the things that make me uncomfortable, or teach in the way that I, myself was taught would also seem like likely paths. However, teaching is not simple. It is not easy. It is a profession where every day is a challenge. It is often a personal struggle. In teaching others, teachers are pushed to re-examine their own thinking and beliefs. The classroom could be used as a forum to teach the ideals of who we would *want* to become. To encompass the humanity and empathy without prejudice. To respect everyone and everything regardless of differences. To form mutual relationships where giving and receiving are the standards. But, it is not just teaching what is simple, what you know, who you are, or what you think "should be." It is finding the delicate balance between these ideas that makes teaching an art. It is knowing how past and present experiences interrelate, knowing which colors to mix on the palate, and when to slow down the fury of the potter's wheel. It is part intuition and part experiment. Teaching is about the ongoing experience. Not the culminating activity. As our list of duties becomes seemingly longer and more complex, I feel that our responsibility in building community bridges remains intact and at the top of the list.

QUESTIONS

For Discussion and Reflection

- How do our first impressions of students influence our ideas about them? How do they influence our emotions?
- Barbara asserts that Thomas did not have relationships established with his peers when school began, and that he grew more and more isolated as time passed. What specific strategies can you brainstorm that Thomas's teachers could have employed to support community building and positive behavior supports?
- How can one-to-one paraprofessionals be integrated into the classroom so that their presence is not polarizing for themselves and/or the student they work with?

In the Field

- In your experiences, have negative interactions between you and a student affected the rest of the students? How have these interactions manifested themselves in the classroom?

- Keep track of negative and positive comments students make to each over the course of a week. Which comments do you think require teacher response and/or intervention?

- Keep track of teachers' responses to peer comments over the course of a week. What are the consequences of the teachers' comments? What can you glean from this about strategic intervention or nonintervention?

- Observe or interview a teacher who is experienced at integrating children who are socially isolated. What strategies can you learn from him/her?

Chapter 4

Scott Howard's Inquiry: Investigating the Challenge of Managing a Classroom Full of Individuals

> *I beg you . . . to have patience with everything unresolved in your heart and try to love the questions themselves as if they were locked rooms or books written in a very foreign language. Don't search for the answers, which could not be given you now, because you would not be able to live them. And the point is, to live everything. Live the questions now, perhaps then, someday far in the future, you will gradually, without ever noticing it, live your way into the answer.*
> —Rainer Maria Rilke, *Letters to a Young Poet* (1994)

At the beginning of my experience as a student teacher, I found myself aiming to control the students with whom I was working. I wanted there to be an understanding between us that I was the one in charge: I was in control. I think I felt that way because I knew that if the class was out of control, and the day was filled with constant interruptions, I would have difficulty actually teaching the lessons I planned. I needed answers to the questions I had about how to be the one in charge. I discovered over time that the questions changed, and my view of managing a class changed. I no longer saw myself in charge of a class, but instead I saw myself as a person leading a group of individuals down a common road. My questions about control morphed into questions about getting to know individual students. My beliefs transitioned from needing to know how to control a class to needing to know the needs of my students, and how to help them feel comfortable in my class. This chapter traces that journey through two main narratives: one from my first student teaching placement in a fourth-grade classroom; the second from my next placement in a first-grade classroom.

PREVENTING CLASSROOM MANAGEMENT DISASTERS

The first time I stood in front of the classroom alone, without my cooperating teacher in sight, I began recognizing the importance behind the process of discovering answers, rather than asking someone to answer my questions. The night before my first day as a fourth-grade substitute teacher I reviewed the lesson plans my cooperating teacher (Ms. Milly) and I worked on together. I envisioned a number of managerial strategies I would use for maintaining order in the class, most of which were variations of strategies implemented by Ms. Milly. I reviewed the material as if I were taking a test that required me to regurgitate some of this information. The next day as I tested a mixture of preconceived notions based on my ideas and my cooperating teacher's suggestions/requests, Ms. Milly's students, who for that day became my students, tested me.

The common phrase that comes to mind for that day is "lost control," as in: "Bill 'lost control' of his car and it hit an embankment." Similarly, "losing control" of one's classroom is not uncommon, nor was it for me on this extraordinary day; a day when fourth graders flew from their chairs, onto their desks and down to the floor with laughter spewing forth from their mouths. A day when the two-person couch became a place of refuge for, oh, say, 15 of the 24 students in the room, all of whom knew the couch was off limits. A day when two students became so frustrated with the comments they were being subjected to by other students, all of which went undetected by me, that they took it upon themselves to leave the classroom and go to the principal's office to inform anyone in the office who would listen. Two students out of the room, and I didn't know they were gone until they returned!

There were points that day that I had no idea what was going on, and the obvious shortcomings of my previous plans became quite apparent when a note was sent back with the students from the office stating that both students should be allowed to leave the classroom for the remainder of the day. Fortunately, the day ended 20 minutes later, and as they left the room, utter defeat crept slowly up my spine. I lowered my head and involuntarily shook it from side to side for one of the last times that day. What—did—I—do—wrong?

MY STUDENT TEACHING PLACEMENTS

In the field component of my teacher education program I was given multiple opportunities to explore this question repeatedly. For an entire academic year, I student taught in two different schools and with three different teachers. Both classrooms I worked in were committed to practices of inclusion; however, the structure of the classrooms were quite different. Ms. Milly's class at P.S. 160 had two different groups of students: those from the local area who had attended the same school since they were in kindergarten and students from the same area who had previously been transported to a self-contained special education school that was part of District 75. This district, as Celia explained in chapter 1, is a segregated school district for students labeled as having moderate and severe disabilities. Under the New Continuum policy, some students who once attended schools in District 75 were being placed into regular education classrooms that offered them access to the "least restrictive environment" (LRE). At this school, this meant that some students were placed in a general education classroom while being pulled out of that classroom periodically throughout the day to work with support specialists. Therefore, while those students in Ms. Milly's class who once attended a school in District 75 were welcomed each morning as members of the classroom community, they left Ms. Milly and the rest of their community members/peers for extended periods of time throughout each day.

My second student teaching placement in Mary and Wilma's class at P.S. 300 was structured differently from my previous experience at P.S. 160. Carine points out in chapter 2 that we worked next door to one another and our classroom environments were similar due to the collaborative coteaching model that the school follows. This model required one general educator, one special educator, and one paraprofessional to manage each classroom at all times. There were a number of students in this class who, like students in Ms. Milly's class, carried labels with them and were deemed "special ed. students" by the school. However, the most obvious difference between the two inclusion classrooms that I worked in at P.S. 160 and P.S. 300 was the amount of support being offered to all students in the classroom on a regular basis. At P.S. 300 I witnessed three adults managing the students in the class differently at all times. It was hard for me to decipher reasons behind which students were receiving help from which adult due to their particular needs. This led me to believe that Mary, Wilma, and Ida (the classroom's paraprofessional) collectively contributed to purposely producing and preserving cohesion among the students in their class, while in Ms. Milly's class it was quite obvious which students had a special education label due to the amount of time they left the classroom to receive outside support/assistance. At both placements, however, as I began recognizing unique differences among the students in each of these classes, I grew into the understanding that *all* students have special needs, not just those who have been labeled as such. By taking interest in all of the students, regardless of their abilities, or behavioral patterns, or anything, I was able to learn more about their precise needs and how to help them manage themselves.

THEORIES AND THOUGHTS ON CLASSROOM MANAGEMENT

One of the coolest and most satisfying realizations I had in college, when I first started volunteering in classrooms and studying (secondary) education, was finding out that teaching involves so much more than just communicating information to a group of individuals. Besides having to assess those people and doing so in a manner that offers insight into their understanding of the information you present to them, an educator must also ensure that he or she has created an environment in which teaching and learning can take place. In order to accomplish this, some educators implement "management theories" (Edwards, 2000). Edwards explains some of these theories and reasons for their usage, in his book *Classroom Discipline and Management* (2000). He writes:

> Teachers who use management theories believe that the behavior of children must be controlled because, they assume, children are unable to adequately monitor and control themselves and because without supervision their behavior will be erratic and potentially destructive. Therefore, teachers must control the students' environment to elicit only desirable behaviors. (p. 19)

Prior to entering Ms. Milly's class as a substitute teacher, I recognized the importance of developing methods for controlling a classroom full of students. However, I also appreciated the idea of self-management, and implementing strategies that would allow my students the opportunity to determine for themselves how best to behave. As Butchart and McEwan (1998) explain, "Teachers are legitimately concerned to maintain basic order. They know full well that there is no learning in a disorderly classroom" (pp. 13–14). In considering how much the students actually learned on October 8, 2001, my first day as a substitute teacher, it is safe to assume that the word "disorderly" understates the condition of Ms. Milly's room. After this experience, I was able to clarify one of my objectives as a student teacher by formulating the following question: How can I maintain order without relying on mere obedience?

While management theories are often "popular and enjoy considerable support in the schools and in other institutions" (Edwards, 2000, p. 19), there are alternatives for managing a classroom full of students. These, according to Edwards, have been labeled "nondirective intervention theories" and teachers who implement practices such as these in their classrooms "provide conditions that promote self-growth and help to clarify life experiences for the individual" (p. 19). Nondirective intervention theorists believe that "intervention in the form of control or directed interaction is unnecessary for children to reach their fullest potential. Children achieve the best possible growth only if they are allowed to direct themselves. From this perspective, children have a natural inclination to learn and become self-directed and self-actualized" (p. 19). Therefore, advocates of nondirective intervention promote the idea that motivation to behave "appropriately" is intrinsic, or contained within the self, as opposed to extrinsic, which would entail motivation stemming from an external force such as a punishment, or a reward.

Likewise, Alfie Kohn (1999), author of numerous works on education and parenting, considers "rewards and punishment [to be] deficient partly because they attempt to control behavior without regard to its cause" (p. 237). He continues by explaining that adults/teachers often assume the reasons behind a student's actions, such as the "obvious" need for attention, and therefore dismiss the logic of asking the student, "What caused you to act in this way?" Even when this is taken into consideration, the tone and wording of the question being asked may elicit a negative reaction from the student. Kohn believes that once the line of questioning is presented in a nonthreatening manner, the student is free to explore the reasoning behind his or her actions. If other "nonaccusatory" questions follow, such as "How do you think we can prevent this from happening again?" or "What do you think we should do now?" Kohn believes the teacher and the student will be more likely to work together on the construction of a plan for the future. Throughout this process the teacher maintains a high level of respect for students by allowing them the chance to explain without feeling like they are being accused.

STUDENTS REQUIRE DIFFERENT TREATMENT

To my way of thinking, Kohn's methodology for assisting a student in understanding the power of choice and self-management is ideal. However, I have found that what is believed to be ideal, just will not work with every student. Instead, each child has a different way of acting and reacting, and even that which I learn to expect is liable to change at any moment. I have been working to learn about the students by acknowledging and reflecting on the questions I have about them. The questions can act as a foundation, which can be referred back to and used in order to produce appropriate responses depending on the student and the situation. These determinations, which often need to be made quickly, can only be made if a teacher knows his or her students, and in making an attempt to do so, recognizes the differing needs among those students; ultimately viewing them as unique individuals that make up a greater whole. Every other person who has contributed to this book expresses that sentiment in her chapter by describing specific differences among students and their needs, whether they are in elementary or graduate school.

Although a classroom is made up of a group of people who are generally in the same age group, it becomes quite apparent to anyone working in one classroom for an extended period of time that age is one of the few characteristics that each student has in common with his or her classmates. Student teaching in classrooms with 20 to 25 unique individuals led me to this understanding and propelled me to question my initial interpretations of the students with whom I worked. I discovered that it is the experiences students have in life, both in and out school, melded together with their natural ways of developing (academically, socially, and behaviorally) that constantly work in conjunction with one another to contribute to the people they are in the classroom.

Something happened when I was in middle school that illustrates one of my realizations as a student teacher. Every year we received different lockers, and one year I learned from a friend that if you count back seven numbers from each of the three numbers that made up your old locker's combination, you had the new "combo" for your old locker. I decided to put my friend's idea to the test and found my old locker later that day. As I was lifting up the lock I decided I didn't need to open the locker itself. I was content knowing that this rumor was actually true. Unfortunately, when I turned around the person who was assigned that locker was standing right behind me. I don't remember what was said at that point, but by the end of that day, or the next, I was sitting in front of both the principal and vice principal being questioned about my actions. I remember being really nervous and pleading that, "Yes, I did open the locker, but no, I didn't even really go inside; I didn't even open the door." They responded by saying, "Well what you did is the same thing as sticking a key in a lock and turning it. That's just as bad, even if you didn't open the door." At the time I had to agree, but now I feel as though their response is bunk. When a person has the key and uses it only to undo the lock, but doesn't go inside, then there is no investigation, and ultimately no discovery. When teachers choose not to investigate the needs of his or her students, they are not using the "keys" they have been given. Every student is like my old locker in middle school. There is a different combination for each and opening the door is a delicate matter.

Figuring Out the Key to Each Student

There is no way to tell exactly what the key is that will unlock the door to learning more about an individual student. There are certain phrases and actions I picked up on during my days as a student teacher that allowed me the opportunity to understand how a teacher might manage an entire class, but learning about the individuals takes time. By the middle of my second semester of student teaching I started to grow impatient, especially after working with three of Wilma and Mary's students: Eric, Matt, and Ned. Depending on the day, they were either best friends or worst enemies, and it seemed as though they hardly ever wanted to listen to me, and didn't care about what I had to say. However, by the end of the semester it felt as though we had all become friends.

This friendship began on a day in late February when one of my cooperating teachers, Mary, suggested I show them how to draw a cartoon character I have been drawing for years (she noticed me doodling the cartoon at various points in class). I did it in steps and they loved it because they each enjoy doodling and drawing. As time passed, we did have the occasional doodling session although I always made an effort to act in the same manner toward them as I would anyone in class. Spending this time with them enabled me to get to know them on a much more personal level. From that point on, knowing every student in the class became a primary goal for the semester.

Soon, I found myself working with many students in the class on things that they showed personal interest in. Many mornings, Sheila, Hillary, and I worked on telling time. While everyone was unpacking their things, the three of us sat in the back of the room for about 5 minutes with an oversized clock. With Morgan, I always talked about his love of snakes, and with Angus about his interest in insects and butterflies. Aaron, however, rarely wanted to talk with me, so we took some time one day to learn about the joys of slapping high fives, and "regular fives," along with "behind-the-back fives." Although I made many conscious efforts with the students, I did not put a check next to their names on an imaginary list. I just did what felt right, and continued doing it if it worked.

I even found out that spending time attending to students' individual interests meant a great deal to children, even when I didn't recall making any special effort. This became clear to me one day while on a field trip. One of the chaperones—Bethany's mother—mentioned to me that her daughter was so excited because I told her she was a poet after reading some of her work one day. Even though it is obvious that we affect people when we are not trying to do so, it was still so surprising to hear. Lucille, the poet's mother, made me realize that it is important to always be positive and encouraging in the classroom because you truly never know *exactly* how you are affecting people until, or unless, you hear about it later.

Some people might criticize this type of attention on student interests as trying to become too friendly with students. For instance, when I was in college, a friend said to me, "Students have enough friends, they need a teacher." That conversation blew open a lot of doors for me. I realized how important it was for me to define that line for myself, between teacher and friend, and as a primary objective fulfill the role of being a great teacher to the best of my abilities. Now I feel as though being friendly with students is an essential ingredient in learning how to be their teacher. Also, I know who I am, and I know being friendly with people and getting to know them is something I love to do, and am comfortable doing. I took the time with Mary and Wilma's students to learn who they each were as people, not just as first graders at P.S. 300. I did this for them, as well as for myself, and by the end of the school year teaching them was much smoother, and my reactions to their actions were more consistent. I was more confident that I was conducting myself in a way that they understood, because I honestly felt like I understood them.

THE CASE OF NED

The following story illustrates my struggles in trying to maintain order and control over one particular student in Wilma and Mary's class (my second placement) long before I had that "confident feeling." I felt comfortable with this particular student, but I did not know how to approach him when he misbehaved during a lesson. It is a story of trial and error, and it was incredibly hard for me to decide what I should do, but I think it is important to reflect on situations such as these as much as possible and talk about them with people who can help. It is important to acknowledge how often I draw from others' managerial strategies and perceive their words and actions as appropriate to model. I handled myself in a similar manner the first time I substitute taught and mimicked many of Ms. Milly's words and actions in an attempt to maintain order in her room. Sometimes other teachers' managerial strategies and techniques work really well for me, and sometimes they don't. It has been important to me to learn what worked for me in each situation, and with each student. Experiences such as these help me understand who I am as an educator and who I strive to become.

On one particular day, approximately 2 weeks after I began my second student teaching placement, in the middle of a math lesson, Ned moved to sit near his friends Eric and Matt, forcing another student out of his spot on the rug. The student who was pushed aside became visibly upset and repeatedly asked Ned to move away. As a result, I walked into the middle of the circle of students and bent down in front of Ned. I whispered that he was not doing the best job he could be doing, and he was hurting the other student's feelings by making him leave his own rug spot. I asked him what he thought he should do right now, and he laughed and said, "Nothing."

My actions and the words were a reflection of those used by my two cooperating teachers, Mary and Wilma, and the class's paraprofessional, Ida.

Since I was new to the class I felt as though using words and strategies that were already effective for the other adults in the classroom would be my best bet in successfully helping the students to "do their best" during lessons. However, I was incorrect in making such an assumption.

I found Ned's initial response to be surprising, because Ned and I seemed to have developed a friendly relationship in the short time that I spent with him and his class. Yet, this was the first time I had taken it upon myself to assist Ned in making the decision to move back to his rug spot and listen to the lesson. Since I was in the middle of the rug and did not know how much I myself was interfering with the students' ability to concentrate, I asked the student whom Ned pushed out of his rug spot to move to where Ned sits normally. I took a seat beside Ned and made many attempts to quiet him down by whispering directions and suggestions as to what he could do to listen and learn. I also spoke to his friends, Eric and Matt, and told them to do their best to use their listening skills to focus on the lesson. The two students were responsive to my request, but their learning was interrupted each time Ned addressed them.

I was sitting there on the floor with the children, and I did not know what to do. I wanted Ned to remain on the rug with his classmates, but it was hard to imagine that that would be the best place for him as he continued to blurt out noises and questions to his friends sitting on the other side of me. His friends had trouble ignoring him and as a result a small group of students on either side of us found it hard to concentrate on the math lesson being presented to them. As Ned became louder, more students began to look in our direction. I wondered if he was listening at all, or just trying to distract his friend and the other students in the class. That was the big question I was grappling with when Ned reached into my pocket and took out a folded up piece of paper containing notes I made during lunch that day.

I didn't notice immediately, but when I recognized what Ned was holding I placed my hand in front of him and asked for it back. At the same time my mind jumped to the thought of a possible power struggle occurring between Ned and me. I knew that teachers should do their best to create a classroom environment in which no power struggles exist between them and their students. Being in a power struggle forces an educator to defend his or her point against a student's argument. I often would be amazed at how my first cooperating teacher, Ms. Milly, would ignore her students if they did not comply with a request she made in the middle of a lesson. For example, students often jumped onto the two-person couch bordering the rug while Ms. Milly was conducting a lesson. Once she requested that people get off the couch on onto the rug, she did not repeat herself, or argue with those students who decided to remain on the couch and not move to the rug. At first I thought she was crazy. How can a teacher let her students get away with not listening, or responding to a blatant request? In time, I learned from my classes that coincided with my student teaching experiences and discovered for myself that: (a) one cannot make inferences regarding whether or not students listen because listening is an internal function and a student's actions do not necessarily reflect whether or not he or she heard what was said, and (b) if the students do not respond to Ms. Milly's request, it was more important for her to continue with the lesson rather than create a power struggle and deter the class's attention from the subject at hand. Eventually I found that Ms. Milly would speak to those students who did not comply with her request once the lesson was over and the class began working individually at their table spots.

In considering Ms. Milly's actions in similar situations I realized that by starting an argument with Ned I would deter his attention from the lesson and create a power struggle between us. I stopped making any request for him to give me back my piece of paper and consciously began the process of ignoring him. I did not know what else to do. I certainly did not want to grab his hand and rip what was rightfully mine away from him. However, as the minutes passed, he began antagonizing me by waving my paper in front of my face and saying, "Ha—haaaaaaa, Ha—haaaaaaaaaa." I remember trying to convince myself that there was no other option but to just catch him off guard, snatch the paper, and put an end to this remarkably annoying frustration. Instead, I sat cross-legged, as still as I could, and kept my mouth shut and my hands to myself. I was making an attempt to model what I perceived to be the best behavior one could exhibit during a lesson.

After a minute or two of taunting, I suggested to Ned that he should be listening to the lesson too, and that his actions were disturbing other students (as well as me) from learning more about the topic at hand. As I began speaking, Ned started to laugh, opened my note, and told me repeatedly, "I don't care, I don't care." I made sure that I said what I felt needed to be said about the importance of being considerate and learning by listening and sitting still, regardless of the fact that he was talking over me, and I purposefully did not acknowledge the piece of paper in his hand until he began carefully tearing it with both hands. I did not want to deal with the situation any longer and whispered to him to hand it back to me, followed with a stern, "Now." Ned laughed and laughed, so loudly that his friends heard and began laughing as well.

That was it. I was sick of it and didn't know what else to do. I didn't want to interrupt the lesson any longer, I didn't want to be laughed at, and I didn't want to see my notes torn apart. I didn't know where Mary and Ida were and I didn't want to ask for help anyway. I felt my ears starting to twitch and heard my own breath being forced in and out, in and out of my nostrils. I felt my back molars grinding against one another just as I snapped at the paper with my hand. Ned did a 180 with his upper body, and now, facing the bookshelf behind us, he delightfully laughed while the piece of paper remained clenched in his tiny hand.

I promptly learned that this was not the best way to handle the situation. "No, no way," was all Ned could say in between spouts of laughter. I ignored him, for about 30 seconds. Then I decided to tell him he had hurt my feelings and I was disappointed in him (again). This, apparently, was cause for even more laughter on Ned's part. At this point, I had to ask myself, "Scott, what exactly are you doing here?" My supervisor, Britt, often asked me to consider what I am trying to accomplish with my actions—what is the objective. I realize now how massively inconsistent I was with my reactions to Ned's actions. At first I was concerned—a bit upset—which smoothly transitioned into an ignoring process that really only riled me up more. From there I became vividly bothered, then angry, and finally, oh yes, now I was hurt *and* disappointed.

Rather than analyze my actions thus far, I started considering what would be the best course of action considering what I knew about Ned. I remember sitting there, slouched over, no longer straight backed and facing forward, but looking down at my lap and feeling defeated. I truly did not want to display my anger and frustration. I thought back to Wilma and Mary carrying, or dragging Ned away from the rug a few times, and each time he was laughing and smiling. I remembered them saying that his sister was communicating with them more often than his mother, and was reminded of how I often observed him waiting until an adult was watching before doing something wrong, such as throwing an object at a person. I decided to jump to the conclusion that he was not receiving enough attention at home.

With this assumption about Ned in mind, I resorted to the only strategy I could think of without neglecting him, or overly emphasizing my disapproval of his actions. Therefore, I told Ned that I was hurt and disappointed in his actions, and reminded him that he should listen to the lesson because it would help him complete his work at his table spot after the lesson. In other words, I said and did exactly what already had not worked for me. I completely forgot what I learned first semester about repeatedly using management strategies that do not work. Ned continued to shake the note in front of me, and as much as I wanted to make any and all attempts to rip it away from him and show him that he is not going to take advantage of me, I stayed focused on the teacher and the lesson. I suddenly became a model student and somewhere, far, far off in my discombobulated mind, I thought maybe Ned would mimic my actions by becoming focused himself, and disinterested in my note.

A couple of solid minutes of complete silence on my part passed and finally Ned returned my notes. I said, "Thank you," and using Ms. Milly's tactic I waited for the lesson to end to speak to him again. I spoke to Ned privately (somewhere in the classroom, but far enough away so the other students could not hear us) about what other courses of action he could take during the next lesson. I did not tell him how he should act, but instead asked him why he thought I was disappointed in his actions during the lesson. He told me he was sorry for taking the note, and I asked, "What could you have done better?" He bobbed his head back and forth and looked at the other students who were going to work in their math notebooks. I told him he had hurt me, and again he said "Sorry," and I asked him what he thinks he should be doing when he sits at the rug. He said, "Listen," and refused to look at me when he spoke even though I was moving my face in front of his to create some sort of eye contact between us.

I remember him starting to move away from me and having no idea whether I should be making any attempts to hold him there or not. I was confused about what to do, and felt as if it didn't matter anyway—that nothing was getting through to him at all. He inched further away so I quickly said, "You should think about how important it is to listen at the rug and stay in your spot on your bottom," He said, "Okay," and ran off to his friends Eric and Matt without first stopping to pick up his math notebook.

I often think about this situation with Ned because I felt so remarkably lost. What exactly went on in this situation, and what would I do if a student acted out in a similar way during one of my lessons in the future and I knew as little about that student as I did about Ned at the time? First and foremost, I do not want there to be a power struggle between the students and me, no matter what the situation. In this instance, with the little I knew about Ned at the time, the best way I could avoid a power struggle was to simply ignore his actions. However, if he was seeking attention his actions may have escalated and he could hurt himself, or other students.

Eventually, Ned did what he felt was best, or correct, but only after I took the time to let the situation settle down, stopped grabbing for my notes, and let Ned make the decision to give back what belonged to me rather than forcing him to do so. In addition, taking this break allowed me the opportunity to simmer down, because I was quite angry with him and frustrated by the idea that I could not find a solution. By allowing myself to become so emotional, I lost control and tried to grab the paper back from him.

I did not know enough about Ned to make an informed decision as to how to handle this situation. In this case, I was guessing what managerial tactics might work best for him depending on what words I knew worked for other people who had known Ned for some time. As a result, I interfered with his, and other students' learning experiences throughout nearly the entire math lesson and assisted in making it difficult for him to understand the work he needed to complete after the lesson was over.

I learned more and more about Ned as the days and months in Mary and Wilma's class moved along. I watched him after hearing directions and information presented to the whole class; frequently, he would make his way from his rug spot to his table spot, and would not know what to do. Mary and Wilma told me he often had trouble retaining information, which made me wonder if there were other ways to present information to Ned other than sitting at the rug, listening, and looking up a chart, or book, or some visual tool being used to convey information.

Ned also presented behavioral challenges to the staff at the school. For instance, there was one day when Karen, the acting supervisor of the school, came into class to assist Wilma in holding Ned down. He was out of control and was running all over the room, knocking things over and stepping on other students. Mary, the class's special education teacher, was sick and there was a substitute filling in for her. The substitute and I were instructed by Karen to take the entire class out of the room while she and Wilma held Ned firmly in place. The substitute and I took the students into the library area of our hallway and we worked with math manipulatives (colored chips, snap cubes, etc.).

Later that afternoon, Wilma and Karen had a meeting, and I was invited to sit in. Karen expressed that she wanted a separate area of the room set up for Ned to go to all the time to do his work. (All the children in the class sat at tables with other students.) Wilma agreed. They also decided that maybe it was time to begin implementing a behavioral management plan. The next day I found out that Mary openly disagreed with Karen and Wilma about creating a separate area in the room devoted to Ned. She did not think he could always spend time on the rug with the other students and that sometimes he would have to be given other small jobs to do to occupy his time, but she adamantly was against putting him in a separate part of the room during independent work time. She did not want him to feel isolated.

I felt the same way Mary did: that putting Ned at his own table would be too isolating. However I did not voice my opinion about it. In addition, I did not ask the questions I wanted to ask for fear of putting myself onto "someone's bad side." This is a moment when, in hindsight, I recognize that I did not learn more about a situation I wanted to discover more about because I was not proactive. I especially wanted to know how Ned would learn anything when he was not at the rug. If he was content doing small jobs such as stacking paper, watering plants, etc., that is wonderful and I was happy if he was happy, but I did wonder when and where he was learning what the rest of the class was learning.

I learned even more about Ned as the weeks went on. I came to the understanding that Ned struggled when attempting to copy illustrations and words from one paper to another. I witnessed Ned acting out against Eric and Matt because he could not draw the same picture they drew and it bothered him so much he ripped up their papers. Had I not known Ned at all and never carefully observed his behavior, I might assume he was simply upsetting two other students. Now that I felt confident in inferring possible reasons behind his actions, I was able to sit and talk with him, and ask him questions that led him to speak a little about why he felt his drawing wasn't good. I also incorporated into the conversation how we could help him work to improve his drawings, as well as develop strategies to help Eric and Matt feel better, and ultimately prevent similar situations from occurring in the future. I discussed with my cooperating teachers what had occurred, and how I viewed the situation. It was in those moments, when I went to my cooperating teachers to discuss what I considered a "new discovery," that I found myself learning the most. Engaging in discussions with Mary, Wilma, and Ida allowed me to formulate a better understanding of how to approach Ned when he would become upset, frustrated, or destructive.

During one of these meetings, I decided—at Mary's prompting—that a fantastic way of getting Ned's attention was to talk to him in a very animated, upbeat way about something that he considered exciting. At the time that I tested this, Ned and Matt were on the same behavioral management plan. Mary told me that the next time I would like to say something to him I should start off the conversation by talking about the sticker he and Matt may get at the end of the day if they behave well. This "sticker business" was definitely exciting news, and therefore, Ned was completely engrossed in the conversation. *Then* I moved on to discuss with him how he might behave a little better in the lunch line and as a result his chances of getting the sticker would improve. He walked away smiling, and didn't try to run away from me once. He also talked to me about some of his options and what he could do to help his classmate, Morgan, feel better after he knocked Morgan's hat off and kicked it to the side.

Throughout the semester I struggled to sort through what I believed about behavior management plans that utilized external reward systems. The idea of extrinsic rewards goes against the suggestions of Alfie Kohn and many theorists who believe in the idea of intrinsic motivation. I noticed that Ned and Matt often would behave appropriately after being reminded about their "prize," but I wondered if this strategy would result in long-term change. Both children filled out their "prize cards" at the beginning of the day by writing in the daily schedule. Then, at the end of lunch and at the end of the day, the students discussed with Mary whether they deserved "smiley faces" for each period of the day. On some days, they did not receive a sticker, and on most of those days there was a serious uproar from both of them. They would often put themselves into the closet and close the door and yell about how upset they were with Mary.

Again, I did not question my teachers about this when I observed the use of the behavioral plan in action. I did not want to insult my cooperating teachers, and felt as though questioning would be an impolite gesture. However, I recognize now that those moments have passed and I did not take full advantage of my situation at the time. I did, however, take advantage of learning more about the students with whom I was interacting with regularly. I learned about Matt and how he often became severely upset with himself when he did not complete a project perfectly. I frequently drew pictures with Matt, and when he did not draw an object or a figure as I did, he crumpled up his paper and threw it out, often crying and telling me that he hated it, and hated himself, and the school. Matt reacted similarly when we performed our class opera for the first time and he realized his mask looked different from the other students' masks. Upon making this discovery, he tried to take off his mask (which was tied snuggly around his head) and rip it up. During one of our group practice sessions Matt refused to take part in singing one of the songs for our opera. Instead of becoming frustrated or upset with his actions, I took him by the hand and led him back to Peter, our class turtle. After we spoke about Peter for a little while, I asked him what was happening at the rug and why he wasn't singing with his classmates. He told me he didn't like doing it. I simply asked, "Why?" and to my surprise, he bent his head slowly to the ground and said very softly, "Because I am bad at it." After a quick talk about how everyone isn't the best at everything, but people still try hard to do their best, he was back at the rug, trying again.

RELYING ON MY OWN VOICE

I am happy to be able to share these stories with a larger audience. As much as I was disappointed in myself at times, and felt defeated, I came to the realization that there are ways of approaching students that no one may ever know because they might not take the time, or have the patience, to learn. I discovered what it means to be "controlling" versus "trying to understand" and I came to many realizations about why students react poorly to those people who respond to their actions in a threatening way. Punishments are said to sometimes backfire, because while they are used in order to decrease a negative action, they often end up reinforcing that behavior even more. I watched as my cooperating teacher, Wilma chased Ned around the room and finally got a hold of him and held onto him while someone went to get Karen. And he was so out of control, and yelling so loudly that we were asked to leave the room—all of us. At one point during the first month of my experience in Wilma and Mary's class, *I* even held Ned close to me while trying to prevent him from running around the carpet. As I held him in a chair off the carpet while Wilma taught her lesson, Ned did his best to step on his classmates' hands sitting beneath us on the rug. He kept pushing backwards with his heels on the floor so hard that we easily ended up 10 feet from where we were when we sat down. He verbally expressed his displeasure and tried to bite my wrists. I stayed calm, said "It's ok, it's alright," over and over again, and thought what I was doing was the only answer, even though it seemed to be making Ned more and more upset.

What I discovered was the more I held onto him, the more Ned suffered. Even though I was attempting to be of assistance to my cooperating teacher, and wanted the class to focus on Wilma and not Ned, I made matters worse by attempting to physically restrain him. Mary was absent on this particular day, and there wasn't a substitute to replace her, which left Ida and me to care for the students while Wilma taught the class. Ida was at lunch, and Wilma made no suggestions verbally, or nonverbally, as to whether or not she wanted my help. I acted on instinct and with little understanding as to how I should approach Ned in this situation. It was not until probably a month later, when finally I said, "Things still are not getting better with Ned; I just don't know what to do." I sat down and had a serious talk with Mary about how best to approach Ned. Not even a half an hour later, I was talking with him excitedly outside the lunch line about his sticker at the end of the day and then about the little boy, Morgan, who was crying in line after he kicked his hat. I learned, but I had to ask, and I couldn't rely on anything but my own voice to get me there.

AN APPROACH TO CLASSROOM MANAGEMENT

One of the more important points that I think I'll need to constantly remind myself of when I become a professional educator is the idea that learning more about my students will be a complex journey full of many layers, a substantial number of which I may never uncover or fully understand. Therefore, I would like to create a forum where my students will feel safe with their classmates and me. My concern is that I will be too strict and allow my expectations for the class as a whole to interfere with, or overshadow the creation of a comfortable classroom atmosphere. As I walked out of Celia's office door late one evening after one of our group meetings, I remember saying, "I just don't know how I am going to be this 'figure of authority' in the classroom." I will never forget her response, which was so simple and quick, "You do not have to be authoritarian in order to be authoritative." I stood there for a minute, pondering her words of wisdom. In order to be authoritative, I think I will need to allow my students the opportunity to choose what is best for them based on the expectations I have set forth in my classroom. Rather than making one choice with no consequence, or another choice with a consequence (e.g., "Oh, looks like you kicked a hat and therefore you chose to be at your own table at the back of the room") Alfie Kohn (1999) suggests giving students the responsibility *to make their own decisions*:

One is repeatedly struck by the absurd spectacle of adults who talk passionately about the need for kids to become 'self-disciplined' and to 'take responsibility for their own behavior'—all the while ordering children around. The
truth is that if we want children to take responsibility for their own behavior,
we must first give them responsibility, and plenty of it. The way a child learns
how to make decisions is by making decisions, not by following directions. (p.
249)

While I will constantly be growing and therefore changing as an educator, keeping in mind that students, regardless of age, are all capable of making decisions that affect their day-to-day life experiences is a lesson I would
appreciate my students being given the opportunity to learn. Kohn (1999)
asks us to consider the possibility of saying, "Something has gone wrong;
what can we do about it?" rather than "You've misbehaved; now here's what
I am going to do to you" (p. 231). We are giving students the chance to be
responsible for the decisions they make now and in the future, by asking
them about their thoughts on a matter, rather than telling them ours. I
strongly feel that students who are given the chance to be responsible are
more likely to develop respect for themselves and in turn, others.

The notion of comprehending how to approach one's students becomes
an enormous challenge for teachers and student teachers alike. The challenge is not in determining answers, but in developing effective approaches
to learning more about individual students. Throughout my student teaching experiences I learned that constructing these nonthreatening, or
nonintrusive approaches while developing a variety of managerial strategies
that prove to be effective, and therefore reliable, is absolutely essential
when one plans on creating a comfortable classroom atmosphere based on
cohesion and consistency. Ultimately, it is the unquestionable promotion
of mutual respect and understanding that I believe helps make meaningful
education possible.

QUESTIONS

For Discussion and Reflection

- What do you think are the differences among "control," "manage-
  ment," and "discipline"?
- What are your beliefs on "planned ignoring" and how did you arrive at
  these beliefs?
- What leads some teachers to draw conclusions such as Scott did about
  Ned not getting enough attention at home? How is this dangerous?

- In your role as a student teacher, how are you dealing with the issue Scott raises about when to ask more questions or be proactive? Do you think it is ever desirable to tell your cooperating teacher you disagree with him/her?
- In this chapter, Scott does not come to a final conclusion about external rewards systems (stickers) and more intrinsic theories of behavior and classroom management. What are some of the specific classroom practices that derive from each theory? When have they been used on and/or by you? What beliefs do you have about each and how did you come to these beliefs?

In the Field

- Observe in a few different classrooms and record the directions (verbatim) that teachers give to their students. After the observation, ask if the teachers will spend 10 to 15 minutes with you explaining their ideas about classroom management. What connections can you start to make between these teachers ideas and their practices?
- Observe and record examples of "planned ignoring." Note the antecedents to the teacher's and student's actions and words, and also note the consequences. Pool your data with other students. What conclusions can you draw from your limited sample? What more data would you need to collect to find out when and if you will use this strategy?

Chapter 5

Leslie Gore's Inquiry: Designing Accessible Instruction

As I was sitting at home one evening, just completing an entry in my student teaching journal, I leaned back and marveled for a few seconds at how I had just written an entire four-page entry about some of my third-grade students continuing to struggle with copying from the blackboard. I went on and on about how many of them copied letter-by-letter rather than word-by-word, or sentence-by-sentence. I wondered if it was all right to be irritated by how long it took them, rather than try to amend the situation. But how much intervention was okay? Would it be better to give them less to copy? To assign copying buddies? Was it ever okay to just do it for them? And was the difficulty some were having something more developmentally or perceptually related? But then it "clicked." The "issue" might have seemed to be solely about students struggling with copying from the board. However, in actuality, I was really trying to reflect on the question of what it takes for a teacher to consciously and deliberately change her practice in order to meet the needs of all learners and to do so in a manner that is respectful of all children and does not compromise her high standards and expectations for all students: what it takes to teach "inclusively." That still remains a very tough question!

I feel as though since my induction into and continuing development throughout the wonderful world of teaching, I have embarked upon a quest for and pursuit of meaningful ways to answer this question. I think it is a question that will continue to challenge me because the answers constantly change as the classroom context and other variables change as well.

I know that I have developed in the sense that I have sought out opportunities to either identify (in the teaching practice of others) or to experience (my own work) the practice of diversifying instruction, integrating assess-ment data to plan for the development of all learners, and evaluating in-struction and finding ways to make it more contextual and relevant, but the journey has not yet ended. The more answers I find, the more questions arise. The more problems solved, the more dilemmas emerge.

We might have heard all the terms and catch phrases before: multilevel in-struction; teaching to diverse learners; instruction for heterogeneity, and so forth. But what does it all mean really? We can try to define the term and phi-losophize about the types of classroom environments we wish to create, but does this guarantee a true understanding of what it looks like and feels like to make instruction truly inclusive? I have found that scratching the proverbial surface of key terms and catch phrases in which I would like to say I believe, and developing a deeper understanding of myself, the values I purport, and the students in my classroom, is very much about "just doing it"—throwing myself head first into the planning, teaching, and assessment of a lesson, or a unit that explores the very things about which I am being theoretical.

I began my teaching career knowing that I wanted to teach inclusively. The journey for me has been about learning to do it and learning to do it well. I needed to experience the physical, emotional, and intellectual work of inclusive teaching. I needed to understand what it was physically like for me to organize multilevel instruction and what it was physically like for my students to become engaged in a lesson that was inherently organized so. I needed to become frustrated and driven by the emotional work of figuring out what was going wrong and what was going incredibly right. What did my emotions and perceptions drive me to do and to *not* do? I also needed to connect this work with other things I was learning. I needed to see it as in-herently part of other theoretical bases and philosophical approaches to which I was also committed.

Future goals and challenges will be to continue to attack each teaching event with the same amount of reflection and enthusiasm. I look forward to finding more ways to answer this question and having more experiences that will challenge and extend my thinking as well as provide a framework for my understanding of inclusive education in general. I hope that this chapter will cause you to laugh, to think and to question, as you reflect about your own self as an inclusive teacher and your own journey toward further enlightenment on Teaching ALL.

DISCOVERING THE HOW-TO'S OF MULTILEVEL INSTRUCTION

Although I truly believed that the most practical part of learning to design instruction inclusively came from classroom experience (or "just doing it"), I still felt as though I needed to expose myself to the available literature about this newfound fascination. I needed to feel grounded in the fact that what I wanted to do was supported by a wonderful, rich research base filled with examples of people who were committed to the same way of teaching. I was just starting out in this field and I figured it would be helpful to consult those who have had somewhat of a head start. Besides, what kind of conscientious graduate student (really frightened by what she had just committed herself to do or to *become*) or provocatively pensive preservice student teacher (often scrutinizing and evaluating everything to the point of *over-analyzation*—a procrastinator's most worthy device) would I be if I did not turn to the one thing without which I could not function or behind which I could probably hide forever: books, theory, research, and more books! Needless to say, I headed to the library in search of my comfort.

I was amazed by all of the great literature that exists about inclusive schooling practices, and specifically, about designing authentic, multilevel instruction. I was fortunate to also have professors, mentors, and supervisors who were able to direct me toward material that ended up becoming quite valuable to me. In fact, I know I will still be referring to much of it in years to come.

What was so useful for me in reviewing much of the literature was that it was literally a plethora of practical information. I appreciated the "key tenets," the "useful strategies," the "helpful suggestions," and the "charts of processes." I would encourage anyone to read these materials and then to actually begin implementing the wide range of possibilities into his or her own teaching practices. In the following sections, I have highlighted some of the literature that has been most helpful for me in trying to reconcile what the world says about designing instruction inclusively with my own values as well as things I have come to know and believe from my own experiences.

To this end, I have also woven into this literature review personal experiences that still exist as poignant memories in my mind. These experiences demonstrate places when this literature became quite real and applicable to me. Each experience is unique and relates to distinct ideas highlighted from the literature. However, as individual as these events were, one day I found myself taking a short break from writing this chapter, staring at the computer screen and trying to find similarities among them. It is in the final section that I extract these larger lessons and themes from the events that seem emblematic of my present understanding of inclusive teaching in general.

COMMUNITY BUILDING WRIT LARGE

Virtually everyone working in the field of education understands (although probably to varying degrees) that their work does not exist inside a vacuum but rather, relies heavily upon cooperation, collaboration, and support. Reviewing the current literature on various models of inclusion, Carine, in chapter 2, highlights an important definition of the word collaboration that embodies the interdependence and joint responsibility that I so much appreciate about a cohesive school and classroom community. I concur with her idea that in order for all children's needs to be met, a *community* must be involved. Jen, in chapter 6, also discusses the importance of building a school community in which all members have agency, while Barbara questions how these wider communities can reach further into the lives of students, promoting their own peer relationships. The idea of collaboration and community is paramount.

It seems almost futile to discuss designing multilevel instruction or creating accessible curriculum without first addressing the fact that, "teaching exists in a context that either supports or hinders effective practice" (Peterson, Hittie, & Tamor, 2002, p. 10). The Whole School Consortium, a group of schools and educators, has documented five major tenets of schooling that I believe teachers might consider in thinking about instruction. They are: empower all citizens in a democracy; include all; teach and adapt for diversity; build community and support learning; and partner with families and the community (Peterson, Beloin, & Gibson, 1998, p. 1).

These guidelines involve integrating social issues with academic learning as well as teaching concepts of social justice; being committed to the ideas that skills and knowledge are often reinforced by interaction with peers, usually peers with differing skills and knowledge from our own; building meaningful activities that are culturally relevant and closely connected to the lives of the students; teaching students to work cooperatively and using other teachers, staff, and community members as valuable resources, creating a safe environment to learn, to work, and to live; and partnering with parents and families to build and strengthen the community.

The idea of community (a community of learners, the classroom community, the school community, the greater, outside community within which the school is situated) becomes quite essential to teachers' work in creating curriculum and truly teaching all. We must not only create opportunities for learning that are supported by this community, but also teach toward the development and maintenance of such a community. McGregor and Vogelsberg's (1998) work on inclusive schooling practices highlights the teacher's role in "creating caring and supportive learning communities" (p. 21). They note that, "A community of learners is an educational setting in which children are encouraged to care about each other and about their learning" (p. 21).

In such communities, there exist teachers and students who are highly esteeming one another and appreciating and celebrating differences. There is a high level of importance placed upon learning together, sharing knowledge, and problem solving. Furthermore, inherent and embedded within classroom work is the teaching of values. Children learn these values through opportunities to work individually and collaboratively, with time to reflect and share about their processes, discoveries, and frustrations.

Through all of this literature, coupled with my own values and experiences, I have learned that the instruction that goes on inside a classroom is very much based on the type of community that the school (including all staff, students, and families) has attempted to build. I truly believe that this plays such a huge role in the type of learning that exists in classrooms. Learning in the context of a strong learning community becomes less of an individual effort and more of a community effort toward promoting understanding and even equity and justice. While this is true, I also realize that too many schools are quite far from this ideal. I believe it is still important for teachers to work tirelessly toward promoting this ideal as best we can, in whatever ways are possible, especially in the contexts of our own classrooms.

I see my personal approach to community building as largely being linked to social studies education. Ronald Takaki, the author of *In a Different Mirror: A History of Multicultural America* (1993), describes social awareness as being able to see ourselves and see history through a re-visioned lens. In turn, social studies education is about this self-awareness, this emerging of a revisionist-oriented, collective psyche, effecting inner change and societal change—for both students and teachers. The purpose of social studies education is thus to communicate the idea of stories touching stories and histories connecting histories. This reflective work, embedded within larger curriculum concepts, brings the classroom community to life.

I have come to believe that students need to be able to: build trust among themselves; work together collaboratively; respect differences; see themselves as valuable parts of classroom community, and in communities outside of school, as constituents with an important voice; and know each other well enough to use each student's talents to discuss challenging issues and organize as a collective in student-centered social action. The role of the school/classroom community is then to: create the type of safe, honest, open, and trustworthy environment where this type of education can be realized to its fullest extent; to teach in a way that relies heavily upon honest discussion, respectful declaration of ideas and opinions and the freedom to wonder and to question; to see community building activities as an ongoing process; and to help students develop critical analyses of communities and provide hope for the possibility of building community in our school and in our world.

Social studies are about developing and changing as human beings, as individuals and as part of a greater community. This development is personal, ongoing, and unavoidable. To commit oneself to teach these studies is a commitment to transfer this development to communal work and understanding within a community of learners. In this way, this development can be more expanded, analyzed, and explored, hopefully toward the betterment of all.

In designing curriculum for my students, through which they can *all* be engaged, I have come to value integrated social studies instruction, through which students may become more aware of themselves and others and through which I can provide, facilitate, and encourage the safety needed to explore the reticent or the feared, the honesty needed to expose the disgraceful and the reprehensible, the openness needed to investigate tacit implications and explicit reactions, and the trust needed to divulge and negotiate the truth about the world around us. My own elementary and middle-school experience was so far from this sort of environment that it was shameful. It is for this reason that I have become determined to embrace and esteem a strong learning community that allows for a building of the type of student and teacher mindset needed to teach all and to teach all well.

Although you might be wondering what all of this has to do with inclusive instruction or teaching all, I have come to understand that community is really at the heart of everything I do in the classroom. Instruction also implies creating a community of learners and creating the type of environment that demonstrates certain values. For all children to learn together and to value each other in the process, a community must be built. Similarly, a teacher cannot effectively instruct diverse learners without understanding that community and without establishing a sense of cohesion within it. Once a strong learning community is established, I believe that designing instruction is made that much easier, and envisioning what it might look like and entail becomes that much more possible.

A CAPACITY APPROACH TO INSTRUCTIONAL PLANNING

One of the most important principles about designing instruction to meet the needs of all learners that I have tried to keep at the forefront of my mind, is that it is more than just about adapting curriculum, or making certain students do more work while other students do less. Peterson, Hittie, and Tamor (2002), in a publication of The Whole School Consortium, note that, "Too often, the adaptations themselves consist merely of watering down, without any serious attempt to address the specific learning needs of the students for whom the adaptations are made" (p. 3). It is also not about individualizing instruction to the point where the teacher is doing something different for each child in her class, a practice that in the zealous attempt to seriously begin addressing some of the existing problems of educational practice, became quite popular in the 1970s (Tomlinson, 1997).

When I took a chance on theory and began to try to create opportunities for authentic learning experiences in the classrooms in which I worked, I concurred more and more with the idea that

> Multi-level teaching involves designing instruction around projects and tasks in such a way that the individual needs of all students are taken into account . . . [This is] a very different way of thinking than trying to build a lesson from the bottom up by starting with discrete target skills and then attempting to address those targets while taking into consideration the individual characteristics of each student. One starts from a holistic, global view and incorporates specific needs. The other starts from specifics and tries to build an overall framework from this. (Peterson, Hittie, & Tamor, 2002, p. 3)

Processing these principles made me realize that it was not enough to maintain the status quo (as far as curriculum, instruction, and lesson planning went) in the classrooms in which I was student teaching, or to simply change around a lesson plan I found so that "struggling students" or "students with disabilities" could merely *participate* in the lesson. I also realized that I could not write a lesson plan asserting that "by the end of a lesson students would be able to . . ." and then attempt to make every student line up with my predetermined goals, especially when the lesson itself did not make room for their obvious needs. After this realization, I then began to ask myself what some of the things were that I *could* do, or what some of the ways were that I *might* effectively design instruction to increasingly incorporate these ideals. I held on to some of the major principles of accessible instruction that inevitably began to frame much of my classroom work.

Oyler (2001) describes planning for student success as having four basic tenets. These tenets are the teacher's keys to making instruction accessible to all of her students. They are: searching for strengths in all learners; expanding beyond the whole class, uniform lesson format; utilizing flexible grouping strategies; and fostering collaborative problem solving.

Searching for strengths in all learners is really about making a commitment to do away with a deficit model for planning for, thinking about, talking about, and evaluating children. This means that a teacher is not so much concerned with what a child *cannot* do, or what a child *is not* as with what a child *can* do, or who a child *is*—what he or she values, loves, is excited by, finds important, or essentially, what that child is really about. The idea here is that knowing this essential information, or making the latter perspective an essential concern, will help a teacher to better see how she can connect the child to the next stage of development while making the child feel valued, respected, and supported in the process.

The Case of Matthew

In my first student teaching placement in a third-grade classroom, I completed a semester-long series of observations of a particular child that culminated in a written child study piece in which I described, through the lens of culturally relevant teaching (Ladson-Billings, 1994), an instructional approach for this child as well as suggested possibilities for teaching him in the area of mathematics. Looking back, I realize that closely observing this child, Matthew, made the study a disciplined effort to search for his strengths and thus plan for his success. I learned that inclusive teaching very much involves taking the time to observe children and to figure out exactly where their strengths lie.

One of the first things I observed during the study was that Matthew had a great deal of energy and was quite excitable. Early in the school year, when the teacher had students draw sections of an autobiographical art piece that demonstrated how they learned best, Matthew drew a picture of his entire body (as opposed to just his hands, or eyes, or ears). The observational data about Matthew seemed to show that he was both very energetic and social in nature.

In one particular observation, I noted that Matthew did not really seem to think that it was always his fault when he started to talk during a lesson because he often talked to the students at his table when he did not "get" something. Matthew often used his peers as sources of information rather than going directly to the teacher. While this was something the teachers probably would have wanted to say they encouraged, he often was penalized for this conversational, social way of learning. Of the Multiple Intelligences, I remember thinking that Matthew might be Interpersonal and Bodily Kinesthetic. Matthew also verbally expressed to me that he got bored with material when he did not understand it.

I came to the conclusion that if social and physical interactions were two of the ways that lent themselves to Matthew's comprehension of material, then teaching could be more relevant to him if it accommodated his style of learning. Over the course of these observations I continually asked myself *how* Matthew was engaged in a lesson or *how* he was paying attention to get a better sense of the type of learner that he was. I recognized that Matthew seemed to maintain his span of attention or level of involvement by doing things that the teachers often misunderstood as a lack of attention and involvement. I saw how tailoring instruction to incorporate these features would probably change teachers' views of Matthew's ability to "pay attention" and to be engaged in the lesson. I also saw how responsibility for creating a relevant context from which students could learn, rested with the teacher. She would fulfill this responsibility by directing attention to her instructional approach.

At first, I wondered why other students could be exuberant, energetic, and social and have people see them as outgoing and personable, but for Matthew, it was the same type of behavior that got him earmarked for disapproval. Then, I realized that perhaps the answer was to create opportunities for Matthew to be successful precisely by using these strong qualities. If searching for the strengths of all learners was a key tenet to making instruction accessible, then if I was able to recognize Matthew's unique essence, personality, and strengths, should I not be better able to plan for and provide instruction for him? I realized that if I truly wanted Matthew to be involved in every lesson that I taught, then I might try creating activities that could not be accomplished without a type of "Matthewesque" participation (social, exuberant, and energetic). By consciously creating opportunities for students to be successful, teachers support them by demonstrating that their own expectations for them are exceptionally high. Teachers should want their students to succeed and so must diversify instruction, perpetually seeking ways and opportunities for this success to unfold.

When I thought about ways that I might plan for Matthew's success in mathematics, I considered much of what I had already been processing. I considered that Matthew might "pay attention" by keeping his body active and that perhaps he was better able to process information when he was bodily engaged. He also responded well to conversational "talk" (where he had a chance to respond and give input rather than be "talked at") and deviations from the routine (like in computer class when he was able to be visually, physically, and mentally engaged all at the same time).

Matthew reported on various occasions that he loved math. In fact he thought it was one of his strongest points academically. Because he did not get the highest grades or complete his work with the most accuracy, his teachers did not give him any reason to think that he might be correct in his thinking. Frankly, I do not believe that our role as teachers is to negatively influence a student's self-perception. There were probably many areas of math in which teachers had yet to discover Matthew's strengths and abilities. I believed he enjoyed thinking logically and could probably be supported in his attempts to do so. Allowing him to talk through problems and perhaps tutor another student who was having trouble seemed like a positive way to support and facilitate his love for the subject, his expert knowledge of certain material, his need for drill or practice of certain content, the building of his own self-confidence, and a pace (of completing work/

figuring out problems) where he had time to think about and evaluate his own work. It also promoted peer-directed talk and conversation, something to which Matthew responded well. Computer math games related to the content the teacher was teaching might have also supported Matthew's need for multisensory stimulation.

Rather than imposing my recommendations on Matthew's teachers in an arrogant attempt to exert the "expertise" characterized by an often critical, analytical, and overzealous (many times ignorant or oblivious to the classroom teacher's thought processes and own methods of reasoning) student teacher, I thought it better to use this information to engage Matthew in many of my own small group math lessons and to remind myself of the importance of making a theoretical "key tenet" a substantial "key practice."

In small group math lessons in which Matthew was involved, I encouraged him to talk through problems with a friend. Many times, Matthew would breeze through a problem, bragging at how "easy" it was. It was during these times that he often made careless mistakes. There were times when he was fully aware of the steps he needed to take to solve the problem, but simply overlooked some of the finer details needed to come to a reasonable solution. For this reason, he became a great tutor/helper to his peers. It was in working with them that he became cognizant of his own mistakes and learned to be more careful in his own work. I was able to help Matthew progress to the next level of development (being more detail oriented in his problem solving) while still affirming his abilities and his love for math.

In other lessons that I was responsible for teaching, I made sure to incorporate activities where students had to walk around and complete physical tasks that helped them to learn new concepts or figure out new problems (i.e., choreographing walking movements to a poem that served as an exploration of where to insert line breaks; and timing what a partner could do in a minute, like how many sit-ups, to get a better perception of how long a minute actually is). In this way, I saw myself providing Matthew, and other students, with different learning modes (different from what was offered on a regular basis) and greater opportunities to express their learning.

This is where I began to make a link between the literature I was reading and what I was actually doing in the classroom. It was somewhat eerie, yet exciting, that the ideas that the literature purported seemed to "jump off the page" (and become much more than just words) when I decided to really consider them seriously. As a student teacher, I think I often feared that I would hypocritically build up a strong theoretical base about education and nothing I truly believed in would ever materialize in my own hands. In other words, I feared that I would only have strong convictions because I read and adopted literature that *seemed* like "sound doctrine" rather than believing strongly about something because of an experience I had from my own work. Then there was also the fear that many of the educational values I possessed would never be practical enough to uphold in the schools and classrooms of the less than idyllic educational system of today.

I was delighted to discover that I was learning by reading, but again, I was also learning, and learning so much more, by doing. I did not always start off deciding to try something out that I agreed with or found interesting from the literature that I read. Often, it was in trying to make sense of what I was or was not doing that I went back to the research, reconciling my own experiences with this literature on inclusive education. In doing this, I was able to change my practice, to give certain practices a name, and in general, to maintain a high level of consciousness and deliberateness about the choices I was making and the ways I was thinking.

There were times when I came home at the end of a long day of student teaching and classes and felt that my mind was racing. I was tired simply from all the thinking! Thinking about teaching and thinking about kids seemed to constantly consume my time . . . and people have the audacity to think that our jobs are easy because they end at 3:00! If I could only get paid for the mental overtime! But nevertheless, the journey continued.

The work of Giangreco and his colleagues (Giangreco & Doyle, 2000) on multilevel instruction presents different possibilities one might consider in planning for curricular modifications. Britt, the supervisor of my student teaching experiences, shared with us a review she had written on the current literature about planning and enacting instruction for diverse populations of students. In this review, she writes of Giangreco's work:

> Here, multilevel instruction in part consists of developing shared educational experiences or activities where students with disabilities may have different or individualized instructional goals within the same curricular area. Another part of understanding multilevel teaching is the practice that is called curriculum overlapping. Curriculum overlapping occurs when individual students have alternative or additional learning objectives in curriculum areas different from those objectives on which other students are focused, but are still engaged in the same learning activity, albeit for different goals. (Hamre, 2003, p. 74)

These possibilities seemed to support the idea that planning for student success is a necessary goal, even if that success means different things for different students.

This possibility still seemed to perpetuate a familiar classroom paradigm where one, more conventional or accepted instructional approach is set against another, more separate approach that is somehow disconnected from the "standard." Still, considering these possibilities opened my mind up to a new way of thinking about planning lessons and gave me a freedom to find strength in those things that during a particular teaching episode seemed to go completely wrong or not according to plan.

LESSON ANALYSIS ONE: *STREGA NONA* AND MATHEMATICS

In talking about teaching and curriculum planning, I have often heard it said that it is tremendously important to create a context, or a whole, from which the "particulars" begin to emerge. In doing so, one can then transition seamlessly to the next step of using particular or specific information to help reinforce, deepen, and reflect upon the context being built. For me, the following lesson I describe was the "particular" that emerged as I was building a framework for understanding accessible instruction. Although the description of it is extensive, I know that the way it will inform my future teaching events will be even greater.

On November 14, 2001 (a date I will never forget), I taught a math lesson to my third-grade students that was the highlight of my student teaching experience. All semester I had been asking questions about the nature of inclusive education. I was concerned about finding and experiencing realistic tools and approaches teachers could use that did not compromise any of the ideals that inclusion purports. I was on a quest for ways to connect theory to practice in the most meaningful and effective way.

After teaching this cooperative math lesson, I was so enthusiastic. I was totally taken aback by the exhilarating experience of being "caught" in a teaching moment during which something clicks and you finally realize that you are doing something right or that things are finally making sense. I believe that true growth in teaching has everything to do with actual classroom experiences and how we respond to these experiences. In effect, as mentioned earlier, the lesson provided a framework for me to direct my questioning and explore the concept of what it really means to plan for the success of *all* learners.

The focus of the lesson was primarily to facilitate students working cooperatively to figure out a math "problem" that was steeped in an overarching understanding of making a schedule (the unit they were working on at the time). It was rooted in a popular story used to motivate and introduce the lesson topic to the children. The ulterior problem that I also wanted students to be working on was exploring the demands and difficulties of cooperative work. Although this was an inclusive classroom, students unfortunately had few opportunities to work together in this way. I saw my role in the classroom as a presence that would offer a different perspective and give them these opportunities often.

My previously described reluctance to assert my opinions and recommendations for Matthew stemmed from my careful attention to not disregard or devalue my cooperating teacher's role in decision making. However, I found that creating opportunities for cooperative work was something that I *could* do. It was a medium that I had quietly negotiated, thus transforming my own role as a student teacher in that classroom. In this simple, yet important way of choosing how *I* might interact with the children, or in what style *I* might choose to teach, I set out to be a doer rather than just an observer. After all, I needed to *do* in order to *become*.

So, for this lesson, I worked very hard to organize the students into heterogeneous groups for the activity part of the lesson. After writing the original lesson plan, I went through the steps pretending to be a student myself, trying to imagine how the episode might go from the experience of the learner. Following the steps of a process of developing multilevel teaching lessons suggested in The Whole School Consortium's publication (Peterson, Hittie, & Tamor, 2002) on multilevel teaching, I then tried the lesson a few more times from the perspective of a few key students in the classroom who I thought might have some particular concerns or difficulties. I made changes and revised the plan, considering anything from materials to transitions to directions.

I read the students the story of *Strega Nona,* by Tomi de Paolo, in which a character, Big Anthony, responsible for doing his chores, instead finds himself overwhelmed by the daunting task of cleaning up a massive amount of spaghetti, a mess he himself created when he disobeyed Strega Nona. After the story, the students and I discussed ways that they personally connected to the book by talking about chores that we do and how long it takes us to complete them. We then turned to a character in the book and made a list of the chores we might imagine him doing. Students suggested amounts of time each activity might take. I then moved into the next phase of the lesson where children collaborated in groups to investigate whether or not this character could finish his chores by a specified time (given a starting time). We talked about things the group might consider such as time for transitions between activities and how fast or slow he was at doing the job.

Before sending students off to work, I spent some time highlighting for them ways the group could work together in order to be most effective. I insisted that all groups had to first *discuss* their plans for a minimum of 5 minutes before beginning to work. I also quickly modeled for them what group behavior, participation, and interaction might look like. As students began to work, I tried to circle the room and facilitate at some points, their group work (many times giving them the *language* of cooperation such as, "Leslie, what do you think?" or "Michelle we haven't heard from you; do you have an idea about . . .").

The sharing time at the end of the lesson was an extremely important way for students to learn about the work they and their classmates had been doing. It also was a tremendous way for me to learn about some very key ideas that one might consider in inclusive education. Students learned that there are many different ways to arrive at the solution to a problem. Each group did such completely different things and learned some really valuable lessons in the process. The lesson emphasized for me the idea that kids can be taught an overarching idea, or "big idea" but can then be actively involved in many *different* ways of putting the idea into practice. Students do not all have to be doing the same thing to be learning similar principles. Nor do each student's learning needs and objectives have to be identical.

I also learned a great deal from my willingness to let this lesson be about a lot more than just math. Students came away from the experience learning such diverse things, some of them seemingly unrelated to math. If I did not let them share these experiences and the things they learned during our share time, I might have done the students and the lesson a disservice. Particularly for one group that struggled with working together and agreeing on a way to simply *do* the problem (they did not arrive at a solution), it was important for me to extract and highlight for the rest of the class what they got out the experience. It was certainly not a wasted effort on their part simply because they did not "get an answer." I wrote down some of what this group shared. They expressed things like, "When working by yourself you can be the boss but you can't be the boss in a group," and, "At first we thought the work would be easy—but everyone has mixed up ideas. The hardest part is coming to agree." One boy even expressed that, "I didn't learn anything except my group likes to argue."

While trying to facilitate this group, I realized that they were learning something just as important as other groups. I tried to help the rest of the class see that if you are attacking a problem with a set of steps to get to the solution, then you will never arrive at a solution if you do not first clarify what these steps actually are. The process has to be organized before the product. What a tremendous thing to take away from a math lesson that was structured socially and embedded with these lessons through an interactive, communicative, and collaborative approach to learning!

This group's, and every other group's experience now became part of a community, or public knowledge bank that made the information accessible to everyone. I believe that it is the teacher's job to mediate these kinds of experiences in the classroom. We often "see" students learning and evidence of knowledge in various forms, however this knowledge often gets privatized. Knowledge becomes accessible when it is made public. Knowledge becoming public also values the learner and the thing being learned no matter what the curricular goals for a particular student. In other words, my goals might be different than your goals, but what we both learn and take away from the experience is equally important.

As a follow-up to this lesson, I began to structure many of my teaching experiences in a way that built upon this tremendous experience. Because my mind was now open to different ways of structuring learning experiences and I felt more free to allow a single teaching event to be about so much more than that one traditional "aim," I felt better able to more deeply consider how to plan for curricular modifications and how to begin designing multilevel learning opportunities for my students.

As I sought to better understand and analyze different teaching episodes through a theoretical framework for talking about, planning for, and implementing inclusive learning/teaching practice, I began to see how I might reorganize these episodes so that specific goals for students could be deliberately chosen beforehand and possibly met throughout. In other words, I might decide, prior to the teaching event that my goal for Kim would be to work on improving her verbal communication skills. If she and her group came away from the event disagreeing and not coming up with an answer to the problem, that is not to say that her specific goals were not still achieved. More and more, I was becoming comfortable with the idea that planning for the needs of various students frequently crossed academic, affective, and physical boundaries. This idea is articulated more fully in the next section.

SUGGESTIONS ON HETEROGENEOUS INSTRUCTION

Again, a Whole School Consortium publication (Peterson, Tamor, Feen, & Silagy, 2002) on multilevel teaching provided me with a practical way of organizing the process of designing accessible instruction. They described the teacher as spending most of her time planning in the areas of academic, emotional–behavioral, and sensory-physical work, and noted that she should thus allow her processes of designing multilevel instruction to interact with these areas. They use the chart in Table 5.1 to depict this point. What was important to extract from this information was that all three areas do not exist independently, but rather, interact constantly. They are flexible areas that the teacher might consider altering or adjusting in order to improve her practice.

This literature, while highlighting thematic learning and interdisciplinary instruction, also sets forth helpful strategies for designing multilevel units and lessons. It suggests, "using three levels of learning goals and roles in learning activities as a way of outlining ranges of learning and different tasks or roles in the learning process" (Peterson, Hittie, & Tamor, 2002, p. 12). Step one is to "identify the learning goals for a unit that you can reasonably expect of your *highest ability student* while bearing in mind the interest, characteristics, and even IEP goals of your lower ability students." Step two is to "design learning activities that help your highest ability students reach this learning goal by either allowing students to (a) work in groups on meaningful tasks taking roles where they can function at different levels of ability or (b) work alone in pairs on related tasks at differing levels of ability." Step three is to "develop additional multi-level learning goals and

TABLE 5.1
Interactions of Authentic, Multilevel Learning
and Individualized Adaptations

	ACADEMIC	EMOTIONAL/ BEHAVIORAL	PHYSICAL
AUTHENTIC, MULTILEVEL LEARNING	Authentic instruction; Project learning; Micro-society; Multiple intelligences	Build community; Promote caring; Encourage friendships; Teach social skills	Heterogeneous grouping; Space for wheelchairs; Use multiple learning modalities
ADAPTING	Advanced projects; Use drama to teach social studies; Provide additional help and support; Read stories to students with reading difficulties	Identify interests; Understand needs and communication; Provide positive alternatives; Peer support; Circles of friends	Talking computer for a blind student; Rearrange books so student in wheelchair can reach them
EVALUATE AND REVISE	Incorporate drama and art into all subjects	Use circles of friends to build community	Use talking computers for all students

Note. From: Peterson, M., Tamor, L., Feen, H., & Silagy, M. (2002). *Learning together well: Lesson about connecting inclusive education to whole school improvement.* Detroit, Michigan: Whole Schooling Consortium, Wayne State University. Retrieved November 6, 2002, from http://www.coe.wayne.edu/CommunityBuilding/WSR%20AToc.html

related tasks/roles in the learning activity," and step four is to "consider individual students with special needs," "check[ing] our initial ideas out with the reality of our students" (Peterson, Hittie, & Tamor, 2002, p. 12).

At the time that I read this literature, what I most appreciated about these steps was that they tried to offer practical ways that a teacher might develop a plan for a lesson. Interestingly, however useful these steps may have been, there was still a certain amount of discomfort I felt when reading them. I recalled B. S. Fennimore's book (assigned for reading in the core course required of all student teachers), *Talk Matters: Refocusing the Language of Public Schooling* (2000), where she writes of negative systems of classifications for students that "tend to name the potential, achievement, and *perceived* value of the students" (p. 20, emphasis added). "The names given to the role and value of individuals construct the social environment of community life" (p. 20). Too often, people consciously and unconsciously accept these names and systems and perceive reality through the warped lenses that these systems provide.

I thought about how difficult it is to even talk about student needs in a direct, practical, yet respectful way. How could I identify the potential of my "highest ability student" when I felt uncomfortable with even classifying him or her as such in the first place? Or how might I address the IEP goals of my "lower ability student" when these IEP classifications were based on a classification system and educational language that in no way embraced democracy or social justice? I knew that having multiple entry points, through which many students could access curriculum was part of the answer. However, was it necessary to name exactly where these entry points began and ended? I am still not sure I have any answers, but I did accept that creating diverse and related tasks and roles in a learning activity was important.

These multiple tasks or roles evident throughout the learning process (addressed by the foregoing steps) are probably most visible in a classroom structure that is characterized by an "organic" flow of instruction. This flow is, "marked by a repeated rhythm of whole-class preparation, review, and sharing, followed by opportunity for individual or small-group exploration, sense-making, extension, and production" (Tomlinson, 1997, p. 9). This rhythm ensures that the teacher can assess students in a variety of ways and design learning experiences based on her best understanding of students' needs and interests. Recognizing these varied approaches made it much easier for me to see a particular student in my fourth-/fifth-grade class at the time, in an important context.

CURRICULUM ANALYSIS ONE:
THE CASE OF ISAAC AND PROJECT TIME

My second semester of student teaching, I was placed in a small, alternative school in a fourth-/fifth-grade classroom. (The entire school was organized around a philosophy that combined-age classrooms more closely reflected natural child development.) This school, or learning in this school, was very much structured around project time, a time for children to explore materials, build models, and try to make sense of the world around them. It was a time for kids to learn many different things in many different ways. The fact that children were pursuing projects of interest to them, sometimes working in groups, sometimes working individually, and that they were working at their own pace, setting their own goals, and meeting different challenges, demonstrated that children were working at many different levels in a way that was quite effective. There were no children who were left "excluded" from the learning happening inside the classroom.

When the entire school engaged in a semester-long study of ancient Egypt, many of the kids' projects became tied to this work. Teachers collaborated to discuss how best to support kids during project time. As I listened in on meeting after meeting, I noted the care taken to allow students the time to discover and to understand the content of this curriculum. They were to learn mostly by inquiry, discovery, and exploration. I watched as kids began to research a plethora of topics related to ancient Egypt, read books, watch videos, talk to others about their knowledge, become jewelry makers and hieroglyph experts, creating their own models of the Rosetta Stone on slabs of clay that they had cut and dried themselves. I watched children build soul houses and tell their own stories of what was inside. I also watched kids become archaeologists, measuring and gridding off pieces of dirt in a sandbox, using fine instruments, to try to better understand the real work that archaeologists do.

This particular child in my classroom, Isaac, made me think long and hard about how project time might be a way to best support some of his needs. Isaac was a student who challenged me. He was a wonderful boy—quite friendly when he wanted to be and extremely energetic. He was also difficult to work with, many times to the point of tears. If you looked at his "records" you would find them smeared with various sorts of information regarding his attention deficit disorder, learning disability, emotional disorders, behavioral problems, and so forth. In class he was often rude and disruptive. At times, it was very hard for him to control his outbursts, both verbal and physical.

Sometimes I was amazed by the ways teachers and staff in the school were willing to work with him, were concerned about him, and were willing to try every new technique under the sun that might work better than old ones. There were different ways that Isaac showed interest in classroom work—especially during project time. But there were other times when I wondered if he was ever really a part of what was going (usually during a meeting on the rug). It was everyone's intention to keep him a part of the community but there were times when he was asked *not* to participate in certain things because of his severe behavior. Multiple entry levels, teaching for heterogeneity—it seemed more difficult when the student himself seemed to distance himself (at times) from the curriculum created for him. I knew that it was important to use and draw strength from what the student did well, but I found myself needing to know how, specifically. I was sure there would inevitably be times when the student would not or could not be part of some activities and I was learning when that would and would not be okay.

One afternoon, as I watched Isaac during project time, something hit me. All semester long I had been questioning how much a part of the school and classroom community he really was. Structuring learning events in which he could be included was sometimes difficult because he was at times out of the classroom—he sometimes worked alone with another adult on a project in a different room. It seemed that he deliberately did things at times that resulted in him being asked to leave a whole group activity and work more individually. At other times, the things he did were not so deliberate. However, Isaac still managed to be very much a part of the class, class decisions, and even class lessons. It hit me that without project time, a very vital entry point into curriculum and community would be taken away from him. Project time, because of the nature of its variability of experience, individual and/or small-group focus, and student–student and student–teacher collaboration, was a time for the many different contexts of this organic flow of varied approaches to be explored. I realized that project time itself had the ability to be the place where I might work to assess, reassess, implement, and reflect upon the learning goals and roles for Isaac as he worked by himself as well as with other students.

As I observed other experienced teachers in the school at project time, I noticed how one particular teacher structured this work time in a way that helped to give students a very clear sense of the purpose of their work and to allow students time to be reflective of their own experiences, learnings, frustrations, and goals. This was evident through a focused work period and time spent recording after project time cleanup. At the beginning of the year, the teacher worked with the students to develop ideas to think about and questions to ask themselves when they came to an ending place in a particular project, as well as questions to think about when they recorded each day. Students had the opportunity to really monitor their own progress and control their own learning experiences. Through my observation, I also learned about the teacher's role as a supporter of the students' work and as one who would make constant efforts to extend students' thinking through questioning.

What I learned from these other teachers was that it was not enough to simply identify learning goals for Isaac, even if they followed every single strategy identified above. Isaac in fact, had to be part of the process of creating these goals in the first place. I needed to hear his voice concerning what he believed he would like to work on, what he was struggling with, and how he could push himself to go further. I understood that he might not always be able to handle an expression of this voice all of the time, but I knew that I need to give him the opportunity. I knew that I needed to help him see that he *could* be successful and that he himself could influence how it was that this might occur.

TEACHING ALL FOR SUCCESS

In reflecting back about each of my student teaching experiences, those included in this chapter, those treasured in the journal I kept and relished from time to time, those so precious and poignant that no written record ever even needs to be made, and those more aptly and eagerly discarded into the frightful sea of forgettable memories, never again to be revisited, I have become increasingly aware of a blatant fact, quite consistent across each experience. There exists a paradox in the idea of teaching all that in order to do it well, it requires getting to know all students well—yet individually. Patterned after the experiences of this chapter, I have contemplated how building communities requires self-awareness as well as the awareness, deep knowledge, and respect of each other (an idea that Scott also relates to his chapter on maintaining flow in the classroom). Discovering the strengths of all learners often means observing individual children in the context of all. Creating curricular adaptations or modifications with the freedom to allow disciplines and goals to overlap involves knowing each child well enough to determine what these goals and meaningful modifications might be. And finally, the necessity of a flow of instruction that utilizes multiple teaching–learning modes implies a respect for the diversity, uniqueness, and needs of individual children.

One does not have to be teaching long to discover that this is an extremely challenging task—especially in a classroom with more than 20 students! I have learned that this requires more work and energy than that to which the average teacher is usually willing to commit. I have also learned that teaching inclusively is really about teaching equitably, and all students deserve a teacher who is willing to put in the "extra" effort. It is a shame that we teachers were never educated this way from the beginning of time (not to mention ever being exposed to the social ills of our society that do all but perpetuate inclusive philosophies) so that we never saw this work as "extra" at all, but rather customary and typical of our lives as teachers.

In getting to know students individually, teachers are better able to organize opportunities for students to learn and to be successful, so that "the seemingly unattainable moves within the learners' reach" (Tomlinson, 1997, p. 17), with the provision of the right support, encouragement, scaffolding, guidance, clarity of expectations set forth and planning. In this way, teachers become "facilitators and mediators of student learning" (McGregor & Vogelsberg, 1998, p. 18). It is the teacher's earnest desire to see each student improve. She is not just content with maintaining the status quo, or with letting each student always do only what they seem able, never setting adequate goals for those students at the furthest ends of spectrum—those who struggle and those who are advanced. With a mindset of knowing *each* to teach *all*, she is about using her students' strengths first, as an approach to confront the weaknesses. She believes that there is *always* room for improvement and it is extremely important for her to help her students realize this about themselves—to encourage them to be metacognitive about their own learning processes (how they process information, what works well for them and what does not, what their next step might be, what possibilities there are to explore, what supports they envision themselves needing, what they can do on their own, how they can improve, where they feel they are struggling, and so on).

This effort to help students become more and more reflective about themselves as learners and about each other is also closely connected to making students deeply involved in the work that a teacher does. After all, one also does not have to be teaching long to discover that making knowledge accessible and creating inclusive teaching–learning environments cannot be efficiently done without the cooperation of students. Students themselves must become the ones to carry on much of the work that the teacher implements. They must begin to initiate their own informal share times where private knowledge is made more public and therefore more accessible. This sharing also helps students to become familiar with each other's work and for teachers to become familiar with students' work, facilitating the effort to know children on an individual basis.

So with this new revelation of the paradoxical element inherent in *teaching all*, not to mention the plethora of new questions perpetuated by continued practice, it is quite safe to say that I have by no means ended this journey of becoming an inclusive teacher. I do not suppose it is a journey that will ever truly end and ironically, there is no race to finish, only the challenge of staying the course. I am grateful for my student teaching experiences because I feel as though I am entering my first year of teaching much more aware. However, I can almost guarantee that I will spend much of my time feeling as though I know nothing at all. I take solace in the fact that there are many teachers, both preservice and in-service, who while on their own journeys, can relate to similar sentiments. So finally, in solidarity with all inclusionistas worldwide, I stand with you and encourage you to—*Stay the Course!*

QUESTIONS

For Discussion and Reflection

- Discuss lessons you have observed or taught that are inherently multi-level and do not require modifications or accommodations for individual learners. What seem to be the reasons for these activities or lessons being accessible to all?
- How have you seen, and/or do you envision, building community through the process and content of the curriculum itself?
- The author writes about "knowing EACH to teach ALL." How is her idea here different from what is known as individualized instruction?

In the Field

- Select three students to carefully observe in different participation structures. Collect their work samples from these observations and analyze what each has been able to accomplish through each different participation structure. What insights does this offer you regarding designing multilevel instruction?

- Identify a teacher who is well known for challenging and supporting all learners in her/his classroom. Ask this teacher to spend 15 minutes with you and explain his/her approach to designing instruction so that all learners are actively engaged. Collate this information with your peers and extrapolate the key principles that these teachers utilize. Compare these principles to the ones that Leslie Gore has identified.

- Select a child either in your classroom or someone else's who seems to be the least connected in one particular curriculum area. Observe the student over the course of a school week. Using the author's framework on finding the strengths in each learner, identify ways to facilitate this student's more active engagement with the curriculum.

Chapter 6

Jen Lee's Inquiry: Struggle and Change in School Communities

This chapter asks the question: What structures support school communities to create inclusive practices? In its simplest form, inclusion is a demographic change in classroom populations; our book focuses on the inclusion of students with disabilities. Taking a wider view, I believe that inclusion has the possibility of transforming education by pushing school culture to support more equitable and inclusive practices for all children. For me, there remains a range of questions concerning how to establish the vision of inclusion in schools; specifically: What do inclusive schools look like? How are resources and services distributed throughout the school? What motivates change in school? These issues continue to puzzle me as we pursue our inquiries as beginning teachers.

GRAPPLING WITH CONFUSION: STUDENT TEACHING, QUESTIONS, AND STRUGGLES

These questions, among so many others, were swimming in my head on my first day of student teaching. The students had not arrived yet, and I was becoming acclimated to my fall semester classroom and school placement. The classroom I was student teaching in was based on the inclusive coteaching model where a special education teacher (Amy), a general education teacher (Eva), and a paraprofessional (Benita) shared one classroom of students. While putting up borders for bulletin boards, I overheard my teachers talking about a student in class. At her daughter's swim class, Eva had run into one of our students, Robin, and her mother. My ears perked up to get some background information on the student. It seems that Robin's mother said to Eva in front of Robin, "I didn't want Robin in the inclusion classroom but I'm okay with it now."

I froze. When I turned around to my teachers, I caught the look Eva and Amy exchanged, a look I interpreted as, "Can you believe this?" Then, Amy said, "I don't understand why they don't allow parents to opt out of the inclusion." I immediately understood the animosity these teachers must have felt from this mother's comment. Her "normal" daughter was placed in the same classroom as "those children": students with disabilities. That day, I rediscovered my naiveté: My most optimistic beliefs that individuals put their "best" interests aside by participating in inclusive classrooms were shattered. I so desperately wanted to see a model of inclusion work!

Right then, I was reminded of how many people make up a school, people with different backgrounds, commitments, and abilities. A school may have staff committed to inclusion but also have opponents from any level, the administration, families, or society at large. With all of these forces in play, how could such a change ever work? Realizing what was at stake here, I was amazed that this school had made a commitment to inclusion by having all parents potentially involved in inclusion, yet I questioned what steps the school was taking to educate parents about the differences of an inclusive environment. Was Margaret implying that it was fairer or just easier to allow families a choice? What message does a school send about inclusion when it gives parents a choice to be in an inclusive classroom? Why weren't all the classrooms inclusive?

Schools have different responses to inclusion and make decisions that affect school organization, the curriculum, and distribution of resources. There are some schools—such as those where Carine, Barbara, Scott, and Leslie student taught—that are small, alternative public schools with a population of students and families that share an investment in inclusive practices in education. These schools base their entire school philosophy on inclusion, heterogeneous grouping, differentiated learning, and equitable distribution of resources. From that first day of student teaching at a large, partially inclusive school, I found myself questioning how inclusion could be successful when individuals within one school have such different opinions about inclusion. With all these different opinions, what can a school do to help build a community that supports inclusive practices and what are our responsibilities as classroom teachers in helping to do this? And then, to what extent does a school community educate itself and its many members about inclusion? Schools may commit to the practice of inclusion, however, in many instances, inclusion is made to fit into old school models rather than taking the opportunity to create new spaces where all students can be successful.

This year, I student taught in two schools in New York City. Both schools had been working toward establishing inclusive classrooms in their schools. In my first placement I saw the coteaching model of inclusion, where Amy, Eva, and Benita taught together. In my second student teaching placement, I was interested in seeing the consultation model of inclusion that had only one classroom teacher, Ms. Milly (who Scott had student taught with the previous semester) and special education services provided to students through push-in and pull-out models. Surprisingly, both schools also had self-contained special education classrooms. Was inclusion successful at these schools? It's complicated and hard to say.

Beyond the Fear of Hopelessness

Ask anyone in the Inclusion Study Group if I had a difficult time writing this chapter, and they would all respond, YES! I am a person who becomes passionate about injustice, and my chapter has been responsible for a lot of confusion, tears, and sleepless nights. The biggest reason for this struggle was constantly thinking about how schools can disenfranchise individuals and then having to put it into words. It hurt to not only recognize the issues, but then they became compounded as I had to remember it, write about it, think about it, and then reflect about it again and again. Writing this chapter tested my strength and hope. I thought about how school becomes a mechanism that undermines the agency of students, educators, and families. Was this the profession I wanted to become a part of?

I have always considered myself an optimist and would often critique educational language as one full of negativity. I was afraid to fall into that same trap in this chapter. Writing this became one of those moments when the struggles in education seemed too big, too embedded into the structures of school and of society to change. When writing, I didn't know where to begin to try to explain what I understood to be many of the obstacles around creating inclusive schools or where to begin trying to resolve these problems. Being a student teacher and not truly a part of a school community made it more difficult: I did not having any agency in the schools I was student teaching and I felt isolated in a role where I couldn't create change. These challenges, however, make me question ways that teachers dedicated to inclusion can advocate for students and help their school become more inclusive. Although this chapter at times depicts disheartening situations, I wanted to include words of hope that encompass some of the spirit of inclusion and the struggle for change.

My experiences differed from the other student teachers in the Inclusion Study Group because before student teaching I had already taught in my own classroom for 2 years. I was in Teach for America (TFA) and taught as an uncertified teacher in a public elementary school in New Orleans. I struggled with teaching and left the profession for a year to work at an educational nonprofit, only to discover I could not leave the classroom behind. Before then, I began thinking about schools while studying public policy in my undergraduate coursework. I brought these experiences in my student teaching observations and my writing.

At times as a TFA teacher and when first returning to the classroom, I felt like a fake. I have had a lot of insecurity returning to the teaching profession after struggling as a classroom teacher. Britt's chapter on supporting student teachers, "Scaffolding Student Teachers' Inquiries," and my own inclusive autobiography later in this chapter will give more insight to what I write here. While teaching in New Orleans, my values concerning education, respect, and student agency were challenged to the point where I became the kind of teacher I despised. There were many times in my classroom where I did not have the maturity, knowledge, or resiliency to create my vision of a caring learning community. As Scott points out in his chapter, "Investigating the Challenge of Managing a Classroom Full of Individuals," I definitely did not have flow and it affected my students in negative ways.

From my experience, I know how difficult it is just to create a *classroom* community, and yet in this chapter, I get greedy and stubbornly want it all by advocating for an inclusive *school* community. As I type, the words may come easily but I know how difficult teaching actually can be, as a new teacher to a new school in a new city and even for veteran teachers teaching in the same school for more than 25 years. But what I have learned by writing this chapter is that despite the struggles this writing provoked, and my struggles as a teacher, I still have hope.

Like many of us say in our chapters, we do not have all the answers, and like in learning, teaching can be filled with a lot of mistakes and pain. It is not surprising that the term *burn-out* is often associated with teaching. I came across the following quote toward the end of my student teaching, and I feel they are words I will still look to after having taught for many years. Herbert Kohl (2001) said in an interview that his advice to new teachers would be this:

> If I were to tell new teachers anything, it would be to function on the basis of hope rather than on optimism. Optimism is a conviction that things will work out for the best. Hope is deep faith that the struggle for things to work out well might eventually succeed. Optimism will almost certainly fail, but hope never dies. (Final section, ¶ 1–2)

The obstacles that may prevent schools from becoming more inclusive communities are just that, obstacles to be overcome. I have faith that our com-

mitment to inclusion will continue to be strong and help create schools for
all children.

WHAT IS THE PURPOSE OF SCHOOL?

Almost everyone in the United States has had the experience of going to
school. Public education has long been a right, regardless of socioeconomic status, ethnicity, gender, religion, sexuality, or disability. I have discovered that any person can feel legitimate responding to and critiquing
education because everyone has been to school. Individuals who have not
stepped into a school in decades, sat at a student desk, or spent more than a
day as a teacher often are responsible for making the educational policies
that affect school communities. Yet school is one of the few places in society
where diverse people must come and work together.

Everyone seems to be invested in education but for different reasons. My
own parents moved from Korea to the United States to have the opportunities that America and education could bring to our family. The potential
must have been that important because we were most likely to have lived a
comfortable life in Korea, yet they chose to come to the United States. Public education, as one of the few means where diverse people come together,
also has had a history of acculturating new immigrants to society's accepted
ways of being. Another purpose of the many purposes for school is that students need to be prepared to be the future of our society. Thus, everyone
has an agenda for schools. What is the purpose of schools then? Is it to
maintain the status quo or to transform society?

I admit I do not have a firm grasp of the theories of school, yet the history of school is filled with the same segregation and inequity reflected in
society: separation by gender, class, race, ethnicity, language, and abilities. I
find it ironic that while education is one of the few rights granted to children (remember they can't vote!), it becomes a place that must respond to
pressures from every legislative and representative level: federal, state, city/
town, school district, and grassroots.

John Dewey (1916), writing about public education at the turn of the
20th century, connects the function of education to notions of democracy.

> The devotion of democracy to education is a familiar fact. . . . A democracy is
> more than a form of government; it is primarily a mode of associated living, of
> conjoint communicated experience. The extension in space of the number of
> individuals who participate in an interest so that each has to refer his own ac-
> tion to that of others to give point and direction to his own, is equivalent to
> the breaking down of those barriers of class, race, and national territory
> which kept men from perceiving the full import of their activity. (p. 87)

Dewey recognizes schools as social places where barriers are broken down, pluralism is embraced, and students grow independently and learn the skills to be members of society. School, then, not only reflects society itself but also is proof of society in the making. It is a place where differences can be recognized and respected. Schools must "break down barriers," and inclusion is the social–political practice that not only can do that for students with disabilities but for all children.

Dewey's quote is particularly powerful in describing the work that schools must do in mediating and respecting differences in students' ethnicities, religions, and political convictions. I was student teaching during the September 11 attacks and remember seeing the school's response a week later: discussion about how the school community could support the Arab-American children and businesses in the neighborhood and a banner in English, Spanish, and Arabic in front of the school. This example brings me back to the question, Is the purpose of school to maintain the status quo or to transform society? Sometimes I am inspired, and other times I am afraid of the answer.

Just as there are different reasons for why people are invested in schools, I have found that there are as many different reasons why individuals work in schools. Realizing that students are individuals and have complex relationships with their families, friends, and neighbors, the "school community" by degrees of separation includes networks of people in, around, and beyond the physical space of the school. Schools must encompass all this in the choices they make regarding school culture, its relationships, language, and practice, yet school staff coming from different philosophies of the meaning of school will differ in their actions and responses. What surprised me in my inquiry on schools and inclusion this year was how prevalent school culture clashed with the ideals of inclusion.

INCLUSION IS NOT JUST ABOUT SPECIAL EDUCATION

The inclusion movement is much more than putting students with disabilities in regular education classrooms. It is a movement that critiques the current education system in our county. Although inclusion comes from the work of Disabilities Rights activists and parents of children with disabilities, I see it as an all-inclusive term that includes all children. Falvey, Givener, and Kimm (1995) define inclusion as

> embracing all, making a commitment to do whatever it takes to provide each student in the community—and each citizen in a democracy—and inalienable right to belong, not to be excluded. Inclusion assumes that living and

learning together is a better way that benefits everyone, not just children who are labeled as having a difference (e.g., gifted, non-English proficient, or disability). (p. 8)

However, schools are often far from being equitable, and inclusion highlights problems that still need to be addressed in schools. Critiques of current special education programs recognize how students, particularly students of color and poor students, have been segregated into a separate systems of education that have not meet the needs of their students (Fennimore, 1997). Inclusion challenges how schools classify students, our expectations for student learning, and the structures upon which schools are based.

Inclusion has the power to transform society by developing new relationships that begin inside a school community and foster mutual respect, compassion, and support for different individuals. Dewey (1900) points out the importance of school movements in affecting society:

> Whenever we have in mind the discussion of a new movement in education, it is especially necessary to take the broader, or social, view. Otherwise, changes in the school institution and tradition will be looked at as the arbitrary interventions of particular teachers, at the worst, transitory fads, and at the best merely improvements in certain details—and this is the plan upon which it is too customary to consider school changes. (p. 7)

There is too much to lose if inclusion becomes only a "transitory fad." For too long schools have segregated students and thus, negatively affected their self-perceptions and opportunities in life. Almost 100 years after Dewey, Thomas Skrtic (1991) writes, "Special education provides the structural and cultural insights that are necessary to begin reconstructing public education for the historical conditions of the twenty-first century and, ultimately, for reconciling it with its democratic ideals" (p. 154). Inclusion, then, has possibility for changing schools.

Robin, the student whose story made such an impression on me the first day of student teaching, was pulled out of our classroom the first week of school. Later that semester, I would see Robin in the yard. All nine of the first-grade classrooms were together in an open space during recess. As the classrooms lined up, I once saw her look at our class. She looked with these wide eyes, observing. What was she thinking about all the students in her previous class? What are her first thoughts about inclusion?

Encountering My Own Biases

What were my first thoughts about inclusion? How did I first learn about issues around inclusion and special education? Although this chapter focuses on the policies, politics, and personal ways that inclusion affects schools, in this section, I describe how I began to develop an inclusive consciousness, particularly in recognizing the rights of students with disabilities. In many ways, I believe that we, as teachers, need to understand our biases and constantly reflect in order to learn and become better teachers. Barbara's chapter ("How Teachers Foster Peer Relationships") spoke deeply to me in how my assumptions affected my classroom practice in New Orleans. Much of our coursework in this preservice program has emphasized the importance of understanding how our own experiences and expectations influence our teaching. You may ask, What does this have to do with creating inclusive practices in schools? In order for a school to become inclusive, I feel that it is necessary that members of a school community—teachers, administrators, staff, students, parents, and the larger community—understand their rationales for inclusion.

Would it make sense to say that there was a time when I was committed to teaching students as individuals but I was not inclusive? I have no recollection of special education throughout school; I attended public schools' gifted and talented programs and also private schools. I can only guess knowing what I know now, that students in special education were probably kept in separate, hidden classrooms—or else, in separate schools. In college, I studied special education in a class on educational policy. Through my coursework, I understood public education as having the potential for social reform and the power to create opportunities for equity. Due to my particular experiences as an Asian American female, I was dedicated to the education of students of color. At that time, I did not necessarily consider the struggles of students with disabilities.

In my Educational Policy seminar, however, I read *Learning Denied* by Denny Taylor (1991). I still remember the book, a narrative of a family's experience with the referral process: Why were schools and professionals saying that this student was failing when there was so much evidence of his ability? I began to recognize the social constructions of disabilities. I was easily sold on the importance of creating instruction that met the needs of the individual learner. Coming from a policy perspective, I had very little understanding of what kinds of reflective planning needed to occur in order for that kind of teaching to take place. In our discussion in that seminar, I remember asking myself, don't we want smaller classes for *all* students? Doesn't every student deserve an individualized education plan?

SPECIAL EDUCATION IN THE PERSONAL: TEACHING IN NEW ORLEANS

When I began teaching in New Orleans, special education went from the abstract to the personal. While I taught in a general education classroom, both of my roommates taught self-contained special education classrooms, one in learning disabilities and one in emotional disabilities. The majority of the Teach for America corps in the greater New Orleans region were special education teachers, filling a great need in the city with the least-experienced teachers. Most of these teachers were in self-contained classrooms with very little support. At home with my roommates, I learned about individual education plans (IEPs), the difficulties of trying to mainstream students, and special education classrooms in the basements of schools. Some of their stories were downright illegal: overfilled special education classrooms, students not receiving the services entitled to them in their IEPs, or IEPs modifications made without parental consent.

In the school where I taught, there were three self-contained classrooms. There was one classroom for third through fifth graders with learning disabilities and emotional disabilities. It did not make sense to me that students with learning disabilities and emotional disabilities were in the same classroom when I was quite certain that these students' needs must be very different. The other two classrooms were for students with physical disabilities. These students were bused in from other neighborhoods in the district. I am still uncertain why, but our school was one of the few in the city that had an elevator to the second and third floors where the general education classrooms were, yet none of these students left the first floor. There was only one child "mainstreamed" to a regular education classroom several afternoons a week during the 2 years I taught at the school, and that child was one of the few White students in special education.

My first year teaching, I was the only teacher in the fourth grade who agreed to have a few students mainstreamed from the third- through fifth-grade special education classroom for math. I tried to speak to the students' special education teacher—who just a few months earlier was the school's gym teacher—about our shared students. We never really talked. He would only say that he trusted my teaching and these students would not be "behavior problems." That really wasn't my concern. I wondered if I was the best teacher for them, if I was meeting their needs, if they were getting a consistent education between our two classrooms, and why their difficulties in math did not look any different than those of other students in my general education classroom.

At the time I was teaching, Louisiana began high stakes testing and our school was the lowest performing elementary school in the city. We then received an extra staff developer from the Louisiana Department of Education. We had some consistency with our acting principal who had made it with us through the year and some changes were implemented. General education class rosters were chosen heterogeneously. Small group instruction became the norm rather than all lessons being designed for whole-class instruction. I had already been teaching the majority of my lessons in small, leveled groups, yet the groups were static based on grade-level abilities.

(Leslie goes further into how this model differs from differentiated instruction, a more inclusive model of teaching in her chapter, "Designing Accessible Instruction".) Unfortunately, one day a month we did not teach but had a practice test in preparation for the standardized tests. Those monthly tests showed how far away our students were from the state standards.

There were a lot of afternoons when I would sit at the coffeehouse with my colleagues discussing what could be done to improve matters for our school and our students. We often spoke about making modifications for our students and whether or not these modifications were working. If they weren't working, did we want to start the process of referring students to special education? It was a double bind of sorts because I saw the self-contained classrooms in the school and in the district overall as "dumping grounds" for students, a place where they would be forever labeled and receive the least resources. But was there a point where modifications were not enough and the student did have a disability? Wasn't this student entitled to services? It wasn't fair that a self-contained special education classroom were our students' only other option.

During the end of my second year teaching in New Orleans, the school psychologist spoke to me quickly about a student referral. After looking at my modifications and spending less than half an hour with Donnell for testing, she said, "He's learning. The tests don't show anything. We want to do everything we can to keep him in the general education classroom. Keep doing what you're doing." I think it was those words when inclusion made sense to me, but at the same time, I felt frustrated because I didn't trust the tests she used and did not know what specifically I needed to continue doing with Donnell, doubting my own teaching abilities.

Those words from the school psychologist, "We want to do everything we can to keep in the general education classroom," upset me because that was when I realized that I had low expectations for Donnell as a student as well as for myself as a teacher. I wanted to give Donnell away to special education because he reminded me of my own inadequacies.

When I would speak to other teachers about making modifications in the classroom, these modifications were often being used as evidence to classify students we were considering for special education rather than for improving the curriculum. The process of identifying a student with a disability was a long, confusing process. A teacher was required to make certain modifications in the classroom for the student and continue with these modifications if they were benefiting students. After collecting data on the student over a period of time and consulting with the Student Academic Team (SAT), the teacher could schedule a meeting with the SAT team and the student's family. The student's family would have to give permission for the students to be tested further to see if there was a discrepancy between the student's I.Q. test and ability.

I understood why some parents would find it difficult to come to school, yet at the time, I really did not understand the politics of labeling. The responses of parents to SAT meetings ran the gamut, from encouragement, to fear, to greed. (During recess I overheard a student bragging about using his "special education check" to buy new sneakers although I am quite certain the money was supposed to support his classified disability.) Unfortunately, very few teachers and schools took the steps to work with families as a student was being classified.

Another teacher once told me that the modifications you presented to the school's SAT team shouldn't be too easy for the student because sometimes it looked like the student was doing fine when in actuality he or she may have a disability. This teacher also said that making these modifications all the time was a really difficult task for just one teacher with a full classroom of students. At that time, I totally agreed with her because Donnell's modifications were a lot of work.

These thoughts are particularly important for me to point out because I brought these experiences with me to my student teaching and future coursework. It is my evidence that a shift of thinking occurred between my 2 years teaching and my student teaching experiences from both being in the classroom with effective, inclusive teachers and engaging in ongoing, focused reflection. I was able to recognize the connections between obstacles that made the inclusion of Donnell in my class more difficult, especially changes needed in my own thinking about teaching and learning.

FACTORS THAT STRUCTURE EQUALITY
OR INEQUALITY

The years between teaching and returning to the classroom have given me the opportunity to reflect on my teaching. Although I came with some knowledge about setting up a classroom of learning, I was excited to be a student teacher because I felt there was still so much I needed to learn in the life-long process of becoming a better teacher. I was able to have the opportunity to step back, versus in the past when I had been totally immersed as a classroom teacher. It was hard to gain perspective then. As a classroom teacher even though I was reflecting all the time, I wasn't able to process the practices at my school and in my classroom with regard to inclusion because I knew very little about special education and learning differences. In New Orleans, I developed a deficit model of disabilities, entering the profession as a teacher with what I thought were high expectations. My story demonstrates the wide spectrum of inclusive consciousness.

As Carine points out in chapter 2, inclusion classrooms come in many forms. The same is true with schools. Both of my student teaching schools struggled with maintaining the spirit and practice of inclusion. As a student teacher, I was able to be an outside observer, committed to teaching my students, learning inclusive practices, and developing an understanding of the complexities of school.

The context around these schools differs, just like the contexts around all schools differ. My first semester school had: academically acceptable test scores; a diverse student population in respect to ethnicity and socioeconomic status; a very involved Parent Association; rich material resources and personnel; and a stable administration. My second semester school: was struggling in test scores; had a higher percentage of bilingual students and first- or second-generation immigrants; a larger Title I population; a gifted and talented program; a bilingual program; and had an interim principal for the last 2 years. Both schools were in different school districts in New York. My questions in the Inclusion Study Group have centered on understanding the cultures of these particular schools in light of how they impede, support, and sustain inclusion.

Who Wants Schools Where All Are Welcome?

Regardless if a school is committed to inclusive change, it still must adhere to district and state standards. How national concerns are interpreted on a local level is the responsibility of the school district and then individual schools. I wonder if the impetus for inclusive schools came from the school communities themselves, rather a regulation for schools, how different the process might be. Even in the same school district, there may be schools with different degrees of inclusion. I have wondered if many of the obstacles I saw in these two schools with regard to administrators' and teachers' commitments to inclusion would be present if the impetus and rationale had come from the school communities themselves? What are the limits of mandated change?

It's like the old proverb: "Give a person a fish, and the person eats today; teach a person to fish, and the person eats forever." Regardless of if and how a school is providing special education services, it does not negate that the law mandating the least restrictive environment (LRE) has been in existence since the signing of the Education for All Handicapped Children Act (EHA), Public Law 94-192, in 1975. Although it has been more than 25 years since the law has been in effect, this top-down policy does not necessarily help schools to become more inclusive. Unfortunately, schools were given a mandate without also being given the support to make the necessary changes in school structures and provide the needed professional development. Who is to keep schools accountable in the name of inclusion— parents, community-based organizations, lawyers, judicial systems, state or local governments, or schools?

How Can One Size Fit All?

The inclusion movement recognizes that there is no single way to teach students and that all students are diverse in many different ways. However, many school practices seem to go against these beliefs. High-stakes testing, student/class organization, and school-wide curriculum are some of the ways I saw school practices go against the ideals of inclusion in trying to make students all learn in the same way.

The pressures of high-stakes testing affect curriculum and cause students to be taught to a particular level with set objectives rather than provide them with differentiated instruction where students' strengths and interests guide curriculum. A significant portion of the spring semester in Ms. Milly's class was spent preparing for and taking the state standardized tests. I remember Ms. Milly telling me that she hated the tests but she had to make the students feel that they could do well on them.

The day of the writing assessment, Amber, a sassy, articulate student in Ms. Milly's class could have done considerably better taping her answers orally instead of writing the required essay. Instead, she did her best on the writing section of the test and shrugged her shoulders when she saw that the test makers provided two blank pages for her response: Her answer only took up half of one page. She finished early and just put her head down for the rest of the test-taking period.

Not only did Amber have difficulties with writing the essay but the content of the essay was nothing she was interested in. Amber would be the same girl who wrote more than eight pages on the life of the singer Aliyah during our May writing unit. Yet the assessment essay asked her whether a crow would be an appropriate New York state bird. Although the students read about crows on the test, how differently could Amber understand the essays if she had grown up seeing them in a suburban or rural setting? Could the messages that Amber received from the test be that her own experiences are not valued and that there is one type of acceptable student? Imagine my anger when 2 months later Ms. Milly received Amber's paperwork from her previous school stating that Amber was entitled to 504 testing accommodations!

I struggle with testing and assessment in their current forms. Although I acknowledge that the government, public, and schools should have an idea of where they stand compared to other schools, unfortunately using norm-referenced tests does not reveal a school's strengths, but only demonstrates how well students performed on this one test. Perhaps, a school has a fabulous arts program, internship program, or strong family involvement programs that other schools could benefit from seeing yet are not revealed through standardized testing. High-stakes testing only recognizes particular strengths, much like gifted and talented programs in schools.

To me, gifted and talented programs seem to be the antithesis of inclusion. The classes are often segregated, static groups of children who have tested well, demonstrated appropriate behaviors, or have had parents advocating for them to be placed in these programs. I had a professor who would say nonchalantly that gifted and talented programs attracted students who can raise test scores and parents who are active in bringing resources to a school. Is that a sufficient rationale for maintaining a segregated and stratified program? On the other hand, teachers who taught in the "gifted" classrooms have told me that their students were no different than the ones in Ms. Milly's and that their teaching practices in these classrooms have not changed.

The allocation of resources to gifted and talented programs could be put toward providing services for all students. At my second school, the gifted and talented program had a paid staff coordinator, and certain programs, like Computer, were only offered to gifted and talented classrooms. In a survey I conducted for my second-semester School Inquiry Project, a teacher in a coteaching inclusive classroom model responded, "Gifted classes often get enrichment programs. Inclusion classes don't get an enrichment or supplemental support program for the entire class." Rather than working toward *both* equal and equitable services, the gifted and talented program created boundaries around resources and students, perfectly mimicking the current realities of society's status quo.

My most disturbing observation about the gifted and talented program was that it divided students racially. A teacher's aide who is Latina and from a bilingual classroom whispered to me about a Dominican student in a general education classroom during standardized testing, "She should be gifted, no? She's smart. She's not in gifted because she's [and pointed to her own brown skin color] not White." The paraprofessional's statement was true: While "gifted" classrooms were ethnically mixed, the majority of White students in the school were placed in gifted and talented classrooms. There were no White children at all in Ms. Milly's classroom.

The students and parents recognized the differences too; a parent responding to my school survey asked, "How can my child be in gifted and talented?" Teachers at the school were also critically aware of the divide caused by the gifted and talented classes; in my survey for my School Inquiry Project, when I presented to teachers the question, "How does the structure of the school—its differently-tracked classrooms—affect the social relationships of the school?" a general education teacher responded that it "separates us [teachers] at times, [and] fosters a strange sense of divisiveness among students." All levels of the school felt the effects of this segregation.

In inclusion, resources for students with disabilities must be redistributed to multiple inclusion classrooms, not merely labeled "special education" classrooms. Some schools like the first school where I student taught, made the commitment and had the funds to provide a large staff of specialists (counselors, ESL instructors, and different therapists). These specialists pulled out students but also pushed into classrooms to provide services for students with IEPs and also students without disabilities but possibly less severe needs. It was wonderful to see these resources for all students and teachers with time scheduled for collaboration.

High-stakes testing or curriculum mandates do not recognize that students learn and develop in different ways. My first student teaching placement had a model of teaching reading and writing skills that Amy and Eva felt was not benefiting all the students. The curriculum revolved around short minilessons and extended amounts of independent reading and writing. Amy, who had been teaching in a self-contained special education classroom for many years, found that many of our students would benefit from having more guided instruction for longer amounts of time. She would also have students cutting out letters, using beans, or manipulatives that reinforced students' preferences for kinesthetic and tactile learning. One student in particular, Mary, excelled in reading when Eva began using letter-sound flashcards and presenting books to her with sentences like "The fat cat sat on a rat."

However, Anita and Eva felt the pressure of staying within the whole school's reading and writing curriculum. The school-wide professional development times were dedicated to literature-based and writing process approaches to literacy teaching. Amy would be especially frustrated after coming from these working meetings because she would hear from other first-grade teachers describing how they had to leave behind students because the teachers felt pressure to not group students homogeneously for skills instruction. Students would only receive 5 to 10 minutes of individualized instruction in conferences with the teacher a few times a week during a daily 45-minute block of independent reading. Although the model provided time for individualized instruction, the instruction was auditory or visual, not repetitive, and not supportive enough for some students.

One response to curriculum that is not inclusive is to pull students out of classrooms for remediation rather than provide that support in the classroom. At Ms. Milly's school, there was only one Resource Room teacher who was responsible for pulling out 40 students and writing their IEPs. Although she wanted to, due to the volume of students she met with daily, she was unable to push-in into classrooms or meet with general education classroom teachers on a regular basis.

The instruction I also planned in New Orleans was usually directed to only one kind of learner. At the time, I didn't understand how my own curriculum could have created additional problems for Donnell in his learning. I wanted to change the student, not my teaching.

How Do You Become a Member
of an Inclusive Community?

When I want to teach something new to students, I try to provide opportunities for new experiences and reflection. In many ways, it feels that teachers who want more inclusive schools need to do the same for themselves, their colleagues, and the rest of their school communities.

At Ms. Milly's school, I would frequently see the same students in the school office waiting to speak to the principal, assistant principal, or guidance counselor. Often, these were the same students from the self-contained special education school district who had been re-registered in their home-zone school. I am guessing that they were always there for behavior problems, but I wonder if the teachers of their classrooms understood how to help a student feel included. In a university course I took on inclusion I read research describing how many teachers are hesitant about inclusion because they do not feel adequately prepared or supported (Shapiro, Miller, Sawka, Gardill, & Handler, 1999).

I admit in my own teaching there were *many* situations when I didn't know how to support a student, and I wonder if I had understood my own biases about disabilities how better prepared I could have been. While I learned a lot in our staff development regarding instruction in New Orleans, I don't remember a lot of opportunities to learn about helping students who were struggling in school other than providing academic and behavioral modifications. These modifications did not necessarily change the classroom but demonstrated how the classroom was not inclusive for them.

Staff development in the schools I student taught in was directed exclusively to practices in the curriculum and offered little opportunity for teachers to share their values or have their beliefs challenged. Grade-level meetings were just summaries of what was going in the individual teachers' classrooms. There was no discussion about effective strategies let alone discussions of one's own philosophical teaching beliefs.

Often teachers' beliefs about their students and about their role as a teacher can be interpreted through their language and choice of words. At Ms. Milly's school, words showed a range of teachers' and administrators' expectations for their students. It was interesting to compare words around "giftedness" and then the rest of the student population. I overheard teachers call fourth graders "kindergartners" and say they were full of "shit." I would less often hear positive statements about these same students. Even questions from other teachers seemed to want negative information because who would want to gossip about a good student? I worried that the students may overhear these statements, perpetuate a language of non-inclusion, and hold low expectations for themselves. I have talked to students when I have heard them use the words "retard" and "gay," but I'm still not sure how to have these kinds of conversations with adults.

Language can be very powerful, and I wonder in the inclusion movement, will there be a time when the word inclusion will not be used any more because all classrooms and the entire school will be inclusive? There have been times when I have felt strange typing the words "inclusive" to describe the classrooms and schools I have student taught in. In some cases, I felt that other school policies negated the classroom from being called inclusive. Yet in other examples, wouldn't saying the classroom is inclusive be separating it from the rest of the school community—when in reality we want all classrooms to be called inclusive? If we had full and true inclusion, there would be no need to differentiate one kind of classroom from another. When other teachers in the school asked me where I was student teaching and I told them, they often responded, "Oh, you're in the inclusion classroom?" as if it was some strange, distant place, as if it were no different than a self-contained special education classroom.

Conversations about roles and responsibilities are needed in order for professionals that were previously segregated to work effectively and collaboratively for student learning. The role of the special education teacher has been changing in dramatic ways. In the past, special education teachers like Amy had their own self-contained classrooms or resource rooms. Now, special education teachers function more as consultants for classroom teachers or are partners in the team-teaching model. In inclusion, both general education teachers and special education teachers must shift their perspectives and responsibilities. It is the special education teacher, however, who is in danger of losing her or his identity as schools move toward coteaching classrooms or collaborative-consultation models. There were times when Amy would say, "I just want my self-contained classroom again." Thus, it is important to have a common vision for inclusion and a community committed to supporting these teachers in their new roles.

As students with disabilities join inclusive classrooms, at times they may need the additional support of a paraprofessional. The paraprofessionals at both of the schools where I student taught felt very underutilized in their positions. Paraprofessionals and teachers also need to support each other's new responsibilities in sharing spaces together. Benita was a wonderful paraprofessional and many times, our first graders did not know she was any different from any of the other teachers in the classroom. It is important to note that other students in the classroom benefit from their presence. As Carine's chapter describes in more detail, paraprofessionals differ in their instructional skills, initiative, and experiences, and must work within the expectations of the classroom teacher. A paraprofessional responding to my school survey said that "the social relationship could be a lot better in this school if people would work together more and not against each other."

In any school it seems inevitable that there will be very different perspectives regarding inclusion until the school the takes the initiative to work toward a vision among all members of the school community about the need for inclusive schools. Simply moving students and resources from one program to another will probably not be effective if the school community does not understand the reasons for change, feel the changes are inequitable, or know how to best support these changes. However, the responsibility for initiating this change rests with the school leadership.

Leadership needs to stand up to pressures against inclusion, help develop a school vision, and support change. However, I do not believe that all school leadership should rest with administrators: It needs to be community-wide and include teachers, staff, parents, and community members. Schools have different models for school leadership. Both of the schools where I student taught had traditional models of school leadership with the principal as the primary leader and different, separate groups for teachers and parents. There are some schools were there are more opportunities for communication among these different groups and teachers have more agency in developing the policies in practice at the school.

Yet it feels as if no one is willing to take the challenge to change school culture. An administrator, responding to my school survey, seemed to indicate that she wanted more community involvement in making school decisions. This administrator wrote, "Beyond being occasionally told that I am doing a good job, I have never been checked up on by collegial, school-wide or district-wide reps" and it would be good to "Maybe give more opportunities for *all* staff to have an active voice in shaping school." Leadership must make school a safe place for all individuals, students, teachers, staff, families, and the surrounding community.

How can schools be more inclusive to students and their families? For many different reasons, parents often feel unwelcome at schools. At the same time, they have their children's best interests at heart and want to advocate for them. Robin's mother, in the beginning of this chapter, most likely felt that she was protecting her child. In order for inclusion to be truly successful, parents must be included in the inclusive process. How can the vision of inclusion be communicated to parents and in turn include parents in the inclusive process at schools? For some parents of special education students, they may be hesitant to have their child be in an inclusive setting because they feel their child may not receive appropriate services or support. These parents' concerns speak directly to the negative stigma attached to the labeling of special education and the inequitable services that many students in special education have received. Rather than use parents as experts of their children, too often parents are undervalued in schools, especially prior to the referral process. In this way, many parents may have no agency in determining the kind of education their child receives, and schools need to consider ways in which they are not inviting to parents, either by language, time, or attitudes. Just in the ways school and teachers must create an environment for inclusion for students with disabilities, they must also create relationships and partnerships with parents in order for the vision of inclusion to be successful.

THE POTENTIAL FOR CHANGE

The many individuals of a school provide multiple perspectives in helping to create inclusive schools. From my observations while student teaching, I have discovered that schools can always be more inclusive in the broadest sense of the word, including student populations, like English language learners or gay students, who are often marginalized by school. Despite the many obstacles for change, there are models to help us build inclusive school communities. Creating inclusive schools is not an easy task: One could argue that it is a dynamic change full of possibility and with no end.

Steps Toward Change: Ideas From the Literature

The importance of building an inclusive classroom has been an important component in our preservice program. Our first readings included Gloria Ladson-Billings' *The Dreamkeepers: Successful Teachers of African American Children* (1994) and Mara Sapon-Shevin's *Because We Can Change the World: A Practical Guide to Building Cooperative, Inclusive Classroom Communities* (1999). Both books primarily presented evidence of teachers practicing inclusive classroom practices, yet the idea of building an inclusive school was short and incorporated into the final chapters of the books. The implicit message I received from our readings was that an inclusive school is created when all teachers had inclusive communities in their own classrooms.

I knew this was a hard argument when I saw the isolation of my cooperating teachers and the attitudes of people opposed to inclusion. As beginning classroom teachers, *when* are questions regarding our role in helping to create inclusive practices at systemic and school-wide levels addressed? Are these even questions teachers are supposed to ask? As teachers are we not supposed to act outside our classrooms? Are the only people who have the credentials for changing schools people who are not in classrooms?

I listen to my colleagues in the Inclusion Study Group and their desires or hesitations to teach at a particular school based on its philosophy and school practices that are already in place. I see the importance of finding a school where one's own commitment to inclusion is acknowledged and re-sources are available to you and your students. Yet I still wonder if all the teachers dedicated to inclusion go to schools that already have programs, who will advocate for students in schools where there continue to be prac-tices of segregation? Will these schools ever become inclusive? If schools are to be examples of society, can we allow any school not to become inclusive?

In my research for this chapter, I read Richard Villa and Jacqueline Thousand's *Creating an Inclusive School* (1995). The book is geared toward educators, parents, and community members and includes the voices of classroom teachers and students with disabilities. Villa and Thousand's chapters provide a framework for better understanding the obstacles I saw in schools that prevented an inclusive school culture. First, they presented different rationales that could move people to change from being an inclu-sion opponent to an inclusion supporter. It made sense to me: Understand-ing my own students' motivations for learning was important to plan more opportunities for teaching. These rationales ranged from the goals of learn-ing, trends in educational research, proof of inclusion working, legal man-dates, funding; and changing your beliefs. The list helped me understand that there can be many ways an individual can be turned to support inclu-sion and knowing the individual is particularly helpful.

I discovered from this list that my own assumptions of inclusion were dif-ferent as I developed my inclusive consciousness. I believe that I was dedi-cated to inclusion first through my commitment to equity and learning. However, in my student teaching, I needed to see examples of inclusion in order to know that inclusion could be done and wasn't some remote theory. I feel that the most difficult rationale for getting people committed to inclu-sion and inclusive schools, is changing our beliefs about and structures for students with disabilities and the nature of public education in America. The assumption that there is only one kind of intelligence that is recognized and embraced in our schools, evident in the popularity of high-stakes testing and gifted education, needs to be challenged. However, for many schools, it seems that legal mandates are what drive current forms of inclusion.

Remember I said I can be really emotional? Thousand and Villa (1995, p. 58) also present a chart that provides insight on the emotional affects of change when schools are pushed to be more inclusive. This chart helped me understand some of the feelings that may make change toward inclu-sion difficult. They determine that the important factors necessary for school change to be vision, skills, incentives, resources, and an action plan. When one of these things is missing, individuals respond with a variety of emotions that affect the process of inclusion—from confusion, anxiety, frustration, resistance, and feeling you are on a treadmill.

In reflecting on my student teaching placements I can see that some of the negative comments I heard from teachers comparing inclusion with their previous settings might be from the frustration that comes from not having resources. For special education teachers who lost their own classrooms to become specialists or to coteach with a general education teacher, they need incentives and the guarantee that the vision of inclusion and their students' lives are not compromised. For myself, I felt a lot of anxiety in my first teaching position because I felt that I did not have all the skills to meet the needs of my students. Schaffner and Buswell (1996) add an important final word to this change process by advising, "Be knowledgeable about the change process, but do not allow it to paralyze you" (p. 59). It seems imperative to remember that obstacles will occur along the process toward inclusion and that change can be a very difficult and emotional experience.

Creating Communities of Dialogue

The isolation and negative expectations that many students with disabilities feel in school are those that teachers may also feel, in their classroom, at their school, and from society. Just as we want classroom communities for our students, shouldn't teachers want the same for themselves in school? Sapon-Shevin's (1999) words resonate with me when she writes:

> We can begin by doing the same things for ourselves as teachers that we try to do for our students: Establish a strong community, develop a solid and reliable support system, set reasonable goals, and celebrate each achievement, not matter how (seemingly) small. (p. 197)

I feel lucky to have had a small community of teachers where I was supported while teaching in New Orleans. I miss those coffeehouse conversations and because our school was designed for open classrooms (no walls), we knew each other's difficult days and could not close the doors (there weren't any!). As a student teacher, I was surprised at how unfriendly schools can be to parents, teachers, staff, administrators, as well as student teachers.

The nature of schools and classrooms can isolate teachers, making it more difficult to create a school community and support each other's growth toward participating in more inclusive schools. In order to create more inclusive schools, there needs to be conversation and safe places as educators and families challenge their assumptions. We need to understand each other's places in developing an inclusive consciousness and each other's rationales for change.

It was an awesome moment for me when the occupational therapists met with Amy and Eva during lunch regarding the students that they saw on a weekly basis and agreed to come into our classroom. When they came, they modeled the fine-motor exercises they used with the students who received services to all our students while also looking for more students that they could support. Among all the teachers there was dialogue, professionalism, and learning. If we recognize the individualism of all our students, there must be a huge range in how to respond to their specific, personal needs. No one teacher will know it all, thus collaboration is necessary.

Advocacy in Schools

Professionalism in teaching is not often taken outside the context of classrooms. However, the role of the teacher must also be in our schools. Teachers are constantly affected by the policies and practices that are laid on schools, yet more often than not teachers do not or are not given the chance to have agency in what happens in our schools. Teachers are not seen as political people, yet we need to be vocal in our commitments. Fennimore (1997) describes advocates as people who should believe that something can be done, that change is possible, and that efforts for children are important whether or not immediate success will be evident. Advocacy, like any effort to change and grow, is developmental in nature, and its social gains are often delayed and later occur out of sight of those who first envisioned them. Often the difficulty of teaching is that progress is not immediate: The planning and work we do as educators have long-term effects that we do not see. Teacher advocates must continue to always have hope.

In order to develop the vision, skills, incentives, resources, and action plans that Thousand and Villa (1995) find necessary to create change in schools, there need to be individuals who are committed to and willing to advocate for inclusion. These do not only include parents or activists, but also teachers. Without advocates for inclusion, there is no force behind the changes that need to occur in schools for inclusion to be successful. Thousand and Villa call these teachers "change agents," individuals who "develop new heroes, rituals, traditions, and symbols that celebrate inclusive practices" (p. 56). In many ways, schools are not expecting teachers to be politically motivated to change schools but in order for there to be change, teachers need to become advocates for their students in their schools despite all their responsibilities inside the classroom. As a beginning teacher, I hope I will first get to know my school community and love it enough to be motivated to help change it for the better.

As student teachers, advocacy can start through being observant and critical about the norms that schools create. It can move toward taking a stand regarding the language that characterizes our students and the assumptions in our society that there is only one, right authoritative answer, in the form of IQ tests, tracking, student segregation, "one correct" approach, method of completion, or response to tasks (Fennimore, 1997). Another way toward advocacy is to understand the procedures, laws, and policies that affect our schools, classrooms, students, and families.

While I respect the possibilities of inclusion, I still wonder if it isn't being done right, is it any better? Which is worse for students, not being allowed membership in a community or being in a group but having no agency in it? Does anyone ask students themselves? During writing one day, Isaac, in Eva and Amy's classroom began to shout at Pia. Amy came to them and when I thought she was finished because she had spoken to Isaac about his yelling, she began to speak to Pia and said, "You can't stand there and let Isaac talk to you like that. You have to say something and tell him it's not okay." Amy's lesson to Pia always helps me to remember that not only do adults need to advocate for students but we must also help students advocate for themselves. Challenging ourselves in this way in our classrooms and our schools is important but it is also important to include other school members and our students—that is how we are able to commit to our values, learn more, and grow as educators.

QUESTIONS

For Discussion and Reflection

- What do you believe is the purpose of schooling? How did you come to these beliefs? Who might disagree with you and why?
- Discuss Jennifer's recommendation that teachers become advocates for children and school change. When have you seen examples of this? What issues have you observed where an advocacy approach might be needed?
- Trace the author's change in her "inclusive consciousness." Make a map of your "inclusive consciousness" and share it with others. What were powerful turning points?

In the Field

- What is the history of special education and inclusion at your school?
- At your school, what school-wide decisions do teachers have input on? Which decisions that affect teachers are made without teachers' input?
- How does your school respond to high-stakes testing?

Chapter 7

Scaffolding Student Teachers' Inquiries: The Vision in Supervision

Britt Hamre

Most student teachers wonder what part the university supervisor will play in their student teaching experience. They often express trepidation and may be thinking: What will my supervisor be like? Will she or he decide if I pass or fail student teaching? Why does an outside person from the university have to come observe me teaching? What will the observation be like? What will I be expected to do? Instead of pondering what the *vision* means in supervision, student teachers may be skeptically mulling, "What's so *super* about supervision?" This chapter explores some of the varying lenses a supervisor brings to the student teachers' classroom experiences and specifically highlights through vignettes how five particular lenses facilitated the growth of the novices whose chapters you have just read.

ENTERING THE WORLD OF STUDENT TEACHING

Within days of beginning student teaching, bonding with the children and cooperating teacher, and diving deeply into the demanding university course work, student teachers often feel simultaneously energized and exhausted. Their lives have become a blend of unending chaos and exuberant joy. Some may still be adjusting to the dawn wake-up calls when caffeine cannot enter their blood stream fast enough. On the other hand, it is not uncommon for student teachers to feel too charged to sleep in their eagerness to see what the next day will bring them; therefore they're awake before the alarm rings. Powerful and sometimes conflicting and overwhelming feelings are typical and have been experienced by countless preservice

115

teachers who have previously entered this always shifting and sometimes tumultuous educational terrain.

It usually takes just a day or two of student teaching before novices come back to campus with a multitude of questions and stories about their teaching experiences. This wide field of experiences may have included arriving home (without realizing how they actually got there) and collapsing on the couch with a positively passionate and exasperated sigh of relief and the knowledge that they love being in the classroom. Perhaps just one child smiled at them and touched their heart in such a way that made all of their (seemingly gigantic) mishaps appear miniscule and unimportant. Maybe they got through to that handful of students who had been struggling with a math concept the day before, or they witnessed the children's eyes light up when they were read a favorite story. While these are special and cherished memories, the same student teacher may have moments—or longer episodes—when she or he feels completely different. They could be pondering whether teaching is the career for them; or asking how they will ever get everything completed on a given day. They may ask, "Will I ever sleep again? And will the children ever listen and respond to me the way they do with their 'real' teacher?" Virtually every student teacher I've known has wondered at some point where their perfectly planned, thought provoking, deeply engaging, creative, hands-on lesson went so pitifully wrong.

If student teachers feel like a pendulum swinging erratically between each furthest point on their emotional continuum, the good (and hopefully comforting) news is that they are not alone! Moreover, there is someone out there that can share their frustrations when they envision falling on their face and likewise applaud them when everything seems to fit right into place. This person is the university supervisor.

SUPERVISION

Much has been written about the role of a university supervisor and preservice teachers' student teaching experiences. In my own experience, and supported in the literature, is the knowledge that preservice teachers view their student teaching practica to be the most valuable aspect of their growth as classroom teachers (Ganser, 1996; Johnston, 1994; Watts, 1987). This experience typically includes a university supervisor. So while the characteristics and requirements of the supervisor will vary from college to college, the student teaching triad continues to be the prevalent model of supervision used today. The three roles consist of the student teacher, cooperating teacher, and college supervisor. In the most effective triads, these three individuals work as a trusted team to provide the student teacher with a meaningful experience (Ganser, 1996).

The significance of an effective triad should not be easily dismissed. Johnston (1994) points that, "collaborative relationships which broaden thinking and provide a safe, supportive environment in which questions can be posed and risks taken will greatly affect the student teaching experience" (p. 81). It seems understandable that those student teachers who experience a close collaborative teaching relationship with their cooperating teacher and supervisor have a markedly more positive view of their time in the field (Johnston, 1994). Likewise, ineffective communication between individuals can greatly hinder the development of a positive and productive relationship for all involved parties.

The Supervisory Experiences of the Inclusion Group

Because the requirements of supervisors vary across universities, I will include here a summary of the responsibilities held by the supervisors at Teachers College. As is the aim of all universities, at Teachers College the supervisor is an important bridge between the university course work and the student teachers' instructional experiences in their classroom placements. The goal of each supervisor is to facilitate a closely knit relationship between the student teacher and cooperating teacher, resulting in a triad where the three members work collaboratively to cultivate optimal growth for the novice teacher. To help foster cohesiveness across student teaching experiences, all supervisors attend a biweekly meeting led by a university professor in the elementary preservice program. At these meetings, we work in small clusters and as an entire group to review supervisory literature, discuss challenging situations, and share strategies to aid in problem solving. It is during these meetings that we also discuss the progress of our student teachers in their particular placements.

Supervisors visit each preservice teacher and observe her or him teach a lesson a minimum of six times over the course of the semester. Visits typically include a short (5–10 minute) preobservation conference where the supervisor and student teacher review the written lesson plan and discuss what will be taught during the observation. (In the beginning of the first semester of student teaching, the novices often start by instructing a small group of children.) The average duration of the lesson is approximately 30 minutes, but will range from 20 minutes to 50 minutes. In most cases, the student teacher and supervisor will arrange to converse about the observed lesson shortly following the teaching event. In my experience the post-observation conference usually starts with the student teacher sharing his or her feelings about the lesson and pointing out specific instances when they felt challenged. Over the years I have found that many student teachers are quick to point out what they see as weaknesses in a given lesson and reluctant to highlight moments when the lesson went well. The postobservation conversation usually includes the supervisor sharing her perception of what transpired during the lesson, recommending some specific strategies, raising a few questions, complimenting a number of successful strategies that were observed, and scheduling a tentative subsequent observation date.

Journal writing is another critical reflection task required of the novices each semester of their student teaching. At Teachers College the supervisors are asked to read and respond to each of their student teachers' journals on a weekly basis. So while the supervisor may only observe direct teaching six times, the journal entries allow the supervisor to understand more fully the unique characteristics of the classroom and become a part of the student teachers' daily experiences. Most supervisors also converse with their preservice teachers over the phone or via email as issues in their placement arise.

In addition to touching base with the cooperating teacher during the six observation visits to the classroom, another responsibility of the university supervisor is to facilitate an assessment conversation with the student teacher and cooperating teacher both at midsemester and during the final days of the student teaching placement. These three-way meetings are typically 30 to 45 minutes in length. Each participant comes to the meeting with her or his comments on an individual copy of the assessment form. During these meetings, and using the completed assessment forms as a guide, each of the participants shares her or his viewpoint of the student teacher's growth in various areas such as classroom management, planning, instruction, professionalism, and collaboration. Toward the end of the meeting the three members collaboratively set goals for the student teacher to work on during the rest of the semester, or in the case of the final assessment, in their next student teaching placement. In the following section I discuss in more depth my personal approach to supervision and the specific strategies I use when observing and communicating with my student teachers.

My Approach to Supervision

Within the basic guidelines delineated for supervisors who work with the elementary preservice program at Teachers College all supervisors have particular approaches they have developed that complement their philosophy of teaching, learning, and management. Here I discuss my general approach to observing student teachers in the contexts of their classrooms. In my own experience as a student teacher, cooperating teacher, and college supervisor, I have witnessed a vast range of approaches to supervision. I have found that most student teachers expect a college supervisor who will sit quietly off to the side of the room observing the lesson and not interacting with either the children or the student teacher for the duration of the lesson. The approach I have adopted is that of a more active participant during the observation. In this case, as the supervisor, I will purposefully engage in the lesson, interacting with the children as appropriate. This is not to say that I help teach or ever interrupt the lesson in any way. Instead, I typically sit with the children on the rug or wherever they were placed and participate with the children when they are working on a specific task. Adopting this approach to supervision creates spaces during some lessons in which I am able to gently model a particular strategy with an individual or small group after the student teacher has attempted several other techniques. Thus, we are able to work collaboratively during any given observation in an effort to support the children in a way that is educative, authentic, and constructive for the student teacher, his or her students, and me.

While the classroom responsibilities and demands on the student teacher increase over the course of the year, my students and I have found it most meaningful when we can schedule our postobservation conference immediately after the lesson. I begin the conversation by asking the student teacher how they think the lesson progressed. In this way, I am trying to create a comfortable place where the student teacher can begin to critically reflect on the experience as I then shift toward assisting them in making connections between the process they undertook in planning the lesson and what actually transpired in the classroom. I use my detailed notes written directly on their lesson plan to facilitate our dialogue. Of course, most of the notes I have feverishly transcribed are not observations exactly, but questions that serve to investigate their deliberate planning, management, and classroom teaching decisions.

Helping Student Teachers Formulate Questions

The hallmark of my approach to supervision includes far more questions than answers. In asking questions of the student teachers I am not "testing" their responses, but pushing them and myself toward fastidiously examining the particular learning experience that took place and recognizing the connections to their early planning and decision-making processes. Critical reflection is thought by many teacher educators to be an imperative stimulus to spur meaningful growth in teaching practice (Cochran-Smith, 1995; Schon, 1983, 1987). By asking questions instead of relying primarily on giving directives or making statements, I am able to gently prod the students toward deeply looking at their teaching and assisting them in thoroughly understanding that every teacher action, word, instructional material, and interaction with the children impacts the learning event in powerful ways. Likewise my questions open up the communication lines and provide me with invaluable insight to what drives their commitments to and process of learning to teach.

The word that frequently begins each question is "why." Why did you choose to group the students in that manner? Why did you choose to sit or stand with, in front of, or behind the children? Why did you choose that book? Why did you use those particular materials? Why did you change gears midsentence? Why were you so intent on sticking with your lesson plan when the momentum of the children and the lesson appeared to veer so far from where you were trying to head? In asking these questions I am trying to reconstruct new understandings with my student teachers about notions of teaching and curriculum. Those of us who have taught in elementary classrooms understand that curriculum is not limited to the subject content taught, but it is the dynamic interaction among the children, teacher, and content (Zumwalt, 1988). Thus, transformative, meaningful learning does not come from memorizing facts transmitted by robotic teachers (unlike so many politicians would have everyone believe). Instead it is a sophisticated, complex, and messy process that involves continual reflection and action.

So while there may not be a "correct answer" to any given inquiry, responding with "I don't know" does indicate to the student teacher and me that deeper analysis and understanding of the complex planning stage in conjunction with the instructional event must take place. As our conversations unfold over the semester trends within the issues we discuss will bubble to the surface. These patterns usually depend on what challenges arise, as well as relate to the varying interests and goals each student teacher, cooperating teacher, and I collaboratively set for their continued growth.

VARYING LENSES

Metaphorically, I have come to see my college supervisory responsibilities as likened to that of a pair of glasses with interchangeable lenses to allow for different foci. My aim is to assist these teachers in becoming adept at looking at their own teaching through various lenses. For instance, we will collaboratively explore their philosophical underpinnings, classroom management techniques, planning, decision-making processes and teaching, and then work to connect those viewpoints and experiences to their university coursework.

Not surprisingly, the lenses that I most often used to highlight each individual teacher's work as a novice overlaps somewhat with their chapter focus. Wrestling with the inner tensions and some painful memories of her past teaching experiences, Jennifer, our only experienced teacher, most often needed to look through the lenses that pointed out the vast number of things going so right in her classroom teaching. Carine's burning question, "What makes a classroom inclusive?" drove our conversations throughout her student teaching experiences as she worked toward teaching inclusively. In my experience, many preservice teachers are consumed (and understandably so) with the day-to-day practical challenges of teaching. My conversations, however, with Carine often took a theoretical and moral bent. Barbara's deep compassion and desire to foster caring friendships between her children was powerful to witness. It was my responsibility to illuminate for Barbara the connection between her own passion to facilitate meaningful relationships between her students and the unnecessarily strained relationship she had with her own cooperating teachers. Scott had an amazing ability to connect personally and authentically with students on an individual level. Pointing Scott toward a lens that viewed, valued, and responded to each child personally within the context of planning, teaching, and managing the whole class became our mutual goal. From the beginning Leslie and I dove headfirst into passionate moral conversations communicating our commitment toward creating inclusive classrooms that we hope will be mirrored in an ever increasingly inclusive world. With this shared perspective, our focus over the semester turned to tying these strong convictions into instructional events.

I would be remiss if I were to insinuate that these lenses are exhaustive of the variety that I used in my efforts to support and challenge my student teachers. In any given observation we often looked at aspects of the lesson through each of these lenses and so many more. In my hopes of creating accessible instruction with each of these student teachers, I found that each person required that I focus on alternative aspects of their growth. Thus we have the variety of lenses. The rest of this chapter is dedicated to briefly exploring each of the student teachers' experiences and my role as their supervisor in connection to these lenses. It is significant to note that these vignettes are not written from my perspective exclusively, but composed of weavings from conversations with the teachers in which I asked them to describe my role as their supervisor, strategies used by me that they found particularly helpful, and moments that were startlingly powerful. The vignettes that follow are written to highlight this questioning nature as I believe that our learning is spurred by the rich questions we ask, ponder, and with which we wrestle as educators and people. My hope is that these questions can be used to stimulate your own thinking and evolution as teachers and teacher educators. Finally, I close with a discussion of my own learning journey.

The Supportive, Encouraging Lens—Jennifer

It is infinitely appropriate that Jennifer came up with the subtitle for my chapter, "The *Vision* in Supervision." I say that because, of the five novices, it was Jennifer who was most in need of seeing her teaching and experiences from an alternative viewpoint, one that revealed the fluidity between her instructional actions, compassionate classroom management, and her deep commitment to equality and equity. For a variety of reasons, Jennifer was initially unable to visualize through her own set of lenses the delicate balance she was striking between creating equitable learning experiences for each individual student, while keeping in mind the educational events that also reached the class as a whole. Jennifer was drowning in an imaginative, yet formidable sea because she was completely dwelling on those moments she perceived as failing. Therefore, she was unable to grasp the larger picture that was coming into focus under her facilitation. It was this broader view of her teaching events that I hoped to illuminate with Jennifer.

> In one particular observation, Jennifer had the whole class of first graders on the floor while she read a book and then engaged them in a discussion about their neighborhood community. From my vantage point the children seemed both excited to share their experiences and knowledge about their neighborhood and attentive to their peers' contributions. Jennifer used a variety of strategies to facilitate the conversation and keep the children's attention toward the discussion topic. Some of these strategies included snapping her fingers, using positive reinforcement ("I love how Wyatt is listening to Samuel."), singing a song to get their attention, playing a noisemaker, and waiting silently to regain their attention. For close to 25 minutes the class was on the floor, listening to the story, talking to their classmates, and engaged in a whole-class conversation. I was completely impressed with the children's attention and Jennifer's ability to keep such young children enthralled for so long. After all, these children are 5 and 6 years old! It is certainly an undertaking to sit in a specific spot on the rug for a solid 25 minutes. Yet, much to my surprise, Jennifer's perception of the observation was vastly different from my own, and she told me so through tears in the hallway during our post-observation discussion.

So what steps did I take to assist Jennifer to utilize a viewpoint that was more open, accurate, and inclusive? The questions I posed to Jennifer hovered around issues of *evidence* to support her perspective. Why do you feel the lesson went so poorly? What evidence have you obtained during the lesson that indicates the children did not understand the concept you taught them? When and how did they appear to be reaching the goals and objectives you delineated for this lesson? How do you know the child that was looking away from you during the minilesson, which was teacher-directed, was not comprehending or even listening to you? Is it understandable if each and every 6-year-old cannot sit perfectly cross-legged for more than 5 or 10 minutes? By discussing these questions (although Jennifer did most of the talking), new understandings were created and her perceptions were modified. It was by allowing Jennifer to talk though her thought processes, decision making, and one-dimensional viewpoint that she was able to construct a new vision for her classroom teaching.

Of course, this is not to say that sometimes a more direct approach did-n't have to be taken with Jennifer. Since she was so tough on herself (this wasn't the only observation that ended in tears), more drastic measures on my part had to be taken. When it came to exploring classroom evidence, I had to almost force Jennifer to see the moments of great cohesion; and there were many. By sharing with Jennifer my vision of those exciting and engaging events she began to see them through her own eyes. She started to understand that she was at the beginning stages of her own growth and learning. Jennifer realized that as a novice it is not only understandable, but also definitely acceptable, if you cannot achieve every last self-imposed goal you have for yourself and the children every second of the school day. Finally, Jennifer made the connection between her own learning journey and that of her children. In this way, just as it is okay if her own classroom children require time to learn additional concepts that are more challeng-ing and complex, teachers also need space to develop the sophisticated skills necessary to teach inclusively. Learning to both support and challenge all learners does not begin and end during your teacher education prepara-tion program. Instead, teaching should be recognized and embraced as a learning process in which your growth and understandings develop over-time through reflection.

The Inclusion Lens—Carine

Carine brought to her student teaching experiences a different set of ques-tions and issues to explore than those of Jennifer. The intense conversa-tions between Carine and me invariably extended beyond the four walls of the classroom and connected to individual and collective discrimination based on broader social norms and values relating to inclusion. Carine, the ever-positive young woman able to look at any disastrous situation and find something educative with which to walk away, became disappointed by her fall student teaching placement. For reasons she could not pinpoint, she just didn't feel like her classroom was what could be described as "inclu-sive." Taking her feelings of frustration and hoping to catapult it into a col-laborative critical exploration, early on a cool Friday morning in Novem-ber, Carine and I visited the school she would eventually student teach at in the spring semester. On our subway ride out to Brooklyn, Carine communi-cated the ideological disconnect she felt with other preservice students that were disinterested in inclusion. I'll never forget the gist of her passionate as-sertion, "I don't get the whole idea that some classes are inclusive and some are not. All classes should be inclusive. Doesn't that mean they include ev-erybody?" On our visit, Carine became invigorated as she stepped into en-gaging and caring classrooms. Finally, she was witnessing truly inclusive classrooms that matched the vision she had created in her mind's eye. From here Carine's focus turned to exploring and identifying what it took to develop and foster equitable inclusive classrooms where each student was unquestionably valued.

Because Carine was so intent on learning to collaboratively create with her children their own inclusive classroom community when she began her teaching career, our dialogues centered squarely on exploring what made both of her student teaching placements feel and look so drastically different. At first it was easy to identify the differences. One classroom had a fulltime general education teacher, a fulltime paraprofessional, and a special educator who visited the classroom a few times a week; whereas, her second classroom was team taught by fulltime special and general educators and assisted by a fulltime paraprofessional. It was too simplistic though, to conclude that the vividly disparate classroom environments could only be a result of these obvious attributes. Exploring specific questions propelled Carine beyond drawing facile conclusions.

My inclusive teaching experiences pushed me to conceptualize "inclusion" as much more than a label slapped on those particular classrooms in which students with disabilities are members. However, I am also cognizant that people must embark on their own learning travels. Thus, I was not going to espouse my perspectives, but rather, wanted to work with Carine as she began her journey toward developing her own understandings about the composition of inclusive learning communities. As part of this joint adventure, I incessantly needled Carine to identify and then investigate those dynamic interactive events between and among the children and adults that contrasted with her previous student teaching placement. It's easy to say the two experiences were radically different, but far more interesting to ponder is the question *why* they were so drastically dissimilar. Carine began to consider why this second classroom experience was so in-line with her own perspectives about inclusion.

Carine explored the following questions and so many more during her second placement. What steps were taken to create this loving, accepting community of learners? What evidence indicates that all children are viewed as precious members of the classroom community? How do the adults speak to and about the children? How do the adults speak with each other? How do the days' events indicate that everyone is valued? How do their actions show that the children are cared for and welcomed? How do these teachers act and speak in ways that communicate their respect, love, and desire to honor the unique qualities of each child? What drives these teachers' every action, thought, and verbal exchange when it comes to their children?

By looking beyond the obvious visual characteristics and by constantly getting into the mode of asking herself questions, Carine came to understand that these teachers entered their classroom with a mindset that each and every child was absolutely and unequivocally accepted and cherished. Moreover, she recognized that if some students were struggling with a particular school learning event, the educators certainly did not blame the student, but used this acknowledgment as the impetus for making meaningful and appropriate change that would end up benefiting everyone. Over time and through this transformative investigative experience Carine came to recognize the foundational beliefs from which her vision of inclusion grew and through which all of her and her cooperating teachers' classroom decisions and interactions stem. At the core was a critique of the notion of normalcy and the realization that this term was not only a mirage, but a social construction created with the expressed purpose of marginalizing individuals deemed different, in this case students labeled as disabled. I think Simi Linton (1998), a disability self-advocate, says it best when she implores, "Inclusion is not an educational plan to benefit disabled children. It is a model for educating all children equitably" (p. 61).

The Relationship Lens—Barbara

Just as Carine developed an understanding that inclusive classrooms could only exist if founded on the belief that excluding even one person makes our communities less valuable, Barbara realized that truly inclusive community must be built on interconnected, fostered, and cherished relationships. Sensing that worthwhile learning events will not occur in a classroom where intimate bonding among the members is absent, Barbara's own desire was to focus on the dynamic interplay that develops among children and teachers. Drawing on her keen observational skills, Barbara was adept at establishing friendly, caring relationships with her students without being perceived by the children as their friend. Finding this balance is among one of the most challenging for novice teachers, since they understandably hope to be loved by the children in their classroom. It almost seems ironic then, that Barbara would have such difficulties during the first part of the semester in developing an open communicative relationship with her cooperating teachers. As mentioned earlier, a close bond between the student and cooperating teachers is a necessary ingredient to having a successful and educative learning student teaching experience. Yet, most preservice educators will feel during their student teaching placements that they are very much visitors stopping by for a brief stay. For one thing, the cooperating teacher will remain long after you complete your student teaching and in all honesty a student teacher is somewhat a visitor in the classroom. So while these feelings are typical there are ways to establish a relationship that will open up classroom spaces where the student teacher is a vital and fully welcomed participant.

As the university supervisor I was able to encourage and strategize with Barbara ways to connect and maintain a positive working relationship between her and her teachers. Student teachers usually enter their placements with an energetic zeal at the thought of having opportunities to try out newly acquired instructional techniques and teach thoughtfully designed curriculum. At the same time cooperating teachers are also adapting to the idea of having an additional person in their classroom and may be contemplating how to fully support a student teacher's growth. As uncomfortable as it was, Barbara forced herself (with a bit of a push from me) to initiate opening the lines of communication, recognizing that she was an agent in her own learning and needed to seize every opportunity possible. It turned out though, that her apprehension about communicating her desires with her teachers to take on more instructional responsibility and a more prominent role in the classroom was completely unfounded.

Early in the semester, Barbara communicated her discomfort when talking with her teachers about her instructional role and desire to acquire additional classroom responsibilities. Barbara specifically expressed concern and dissatisfaction with the number of opportunities to develop long-range curriculum experiences for the whole class. Simply put, Barbara was hoping to take on more instructional and planning responsibilities. Again, as with Jennifer and Carine the questions I posed invited Barbara to share with me *evidence* as to "why" she felt isolated and expendable in the classroom teaching team. Next I posited to Barbara questions to spur strategic ideas to get those communicative lines flowing. What ways have you initiated talking to your teachers about the kinds of teaching experiences you would like to have? When are times during the course of the day that you have the opportunity to speak privately with your teachers? Are there times during the day that the teachers seem more relaxed and less pressed for time? Can you pinpoint times during typical conversation courses that you could naturally insert some ideas about the instructional responsibilities you'd like to take over, as opposed to making your requests a major focal topic? What makes you think that the teachers wouldn't be open, willing, and even thrilled that you would like to take on additional teaching responsibilities? By conversing together, and exploring Barbara's answers to these questions we were able to brainstorm a plethora of times, approaches, and conversational starters where she could communicate her concerns during the interactions Barbara was already having with her teachers. And although this initiation caused Barbara's heart to race just a bit, in the end it turned out that her teachers had actually thought they were doing her a favor by not loading her down with so many responsibilities.

So even though I only visited Barbara eight times over the course of the semester, I was able to play a significant role in the relationship she developed with her cooperating teacher. Student teachers may feel that their supervisors have limited influence on their student teaching placements, and in some instances that may be true. However, if the supervisor and student teacher both make a valiant effort to communicate openly as issues arise, the supervisor can be a critical resource—able to support, strategize, and collaborate with the student teacher. Then, if all else fails, the supervisor can also be an invaluable liaison, intervening on the part of the student teacher. What I've come to learn over the years, and as Barbara also came to see, is that intervention of this sort is largely unnecessary when student teachers take it upon themselves to take a tiny chance and share their thoughts and feelings with their cooperating teachers.

The Management Lens—Scott

When working with Scott during his spring semester of student teaching, my lens again took a different focus. One might assume it would be impossible to walk into a first-grade classroom and not immediately notice the tall lanky blond man interacting with the children. However, it was just this situation that I found myself in during the first few times visiting Scott. After a moment I would locate him deeply involved in a conversation, book, or playing an educational game with one or more children. Scott's ability to connect so meaningfully with the students on a personal level was truly amazing to witness and made him—just for a second—unidentifiable among the children. However, it was Scott's difficulty managing the whole classroom that presented us with the most formidable challenge of the semester. This assertion didn't just come from me; from the beginning of our tenure working together Scott was brutally honest about his struggle with classroom management. Scott's recognition was nothing earth-shattering to me; after all, wrestling with managing a classroom of diverse, energetic young students is among the most cited concerns of novice teachers (Ganser, 1996). Learning to manage the whole class and address challenging student behavior was only part of the picture representing Scott's remarkable journey of growth.

In one of the first lessons I observed, Scott found himself particularly challenged by managing the children while teaching a math concept with several manipulatives. Scott started by having the students sit on the floor in a circle with him at the front near the board. Committed to providing instruction that required the students' active participation, he next chose students to help him demonstrate the concept of "greater than" and "less than." Instructing these five students to come into the circle, he gave them two bags holding different quantities of math cubes and asked them to pour them out and determine which bag had a greater amount and which bag had a lesser number. Since the rest of the class could not see the process the five students were engaging in (the students in the middle were huddling together to count the pieces) they proceeded to stand up, push peers out of the way initiate conversations that were unrelated to the math activity. Scott recognized that the rest of the class was distracted and losing attention and worked to remedy the situation by having another group of student start the next example using a scale to compare the weights of two different objects. Once this small group (also on the small carpet) started completing their task, still other students were not sure of where to focus: the first group of students or second. This created another wave of activity unrelated to the math concept and the voices and physical activity of the children began to rise.

Trying to take "control" of the situation, Scott stopped everything and (with the help of his cooperating teachers) was successful in getting the students to return to their original floor spaces. Instead of sticking with these two activities, Scott began a completely different example that he thought of on the spot. After this one example of comparing the number of markers in his two hands to determine which was the greater amount, Scott turned his back on the group of students and wrote the symbols for these math concepts (> and <) on the board. Unfortunately the first three dry erase markers he chose were completely dry, and in response to the delay the children started chattering with their neighbors. After verbally explaining the meaning and use for each symbol, Scott asked students one by one to come to him and get their math workbooks, find a seat around the room and begin completing page 46. Students broke out in conversation once again, but this time it was to say, "What do we have to do?" or "I don't understand" or "Where do we sit?" Stepping in again to help transition the children to this individual task, Scott's cooperating teachers began directing students to specific seating spaces and roaming the room to assist the children in this workbook page.

As evidenced by this short example, coupled with his initial inability to consistently manage a classroom of children was Scott's early ineptitude in planning and teaching a cohesive lesson where the students grasped the academic content and were able to engage in the activity. Thankfully, what I came to understand early on in the semester was that Scott had never really been taught, step by miniscule step, what comprises a succinctly planned lesson and how to put those pieces together on his own. Scott forced me out of my comfortable approach of being a facilitator who asked a never-ending list of questions and required me to be more direct in my guidance. This is not to say that the questions ever stopped: At one point I actually gave him a three-page typed list of questions to reference when planning. Yet, there came a time the first week of March when I had to sit down with Scott and explicitly and supportively communicate my significant concerns about his progress thus far in the semester. Afterward, Scott (on several occasions) told me that my painfully honest assessment was exactly the swift "kick in the pants" he needed to see the reality of his situation, refocus his attention, and get serious about embarking on his chosen career path. Teachers realize over time how intricately these two critical issues—planning tightly constructed lessons and managing a classroom full of individuals—are fused together. It was my charge to insure that Scott came to understand this interwoven connection.

With our collective goals lighting the way, we worked to identify the tenets of a planning approach and management strategies that Scott felt aligned with his vision of teaching. Initially Scott did not comprehend the absolute necessity in understanding *why* he was making the decisions he was making in his planning, teaching, and management of the children. At one of our first collaborative planning sessions, I fired questions in response to Scott's every statement about what he had planned for a subsequent observation. Invariably, my inquiries began with "why." Why did you choose that goal and those objectives? Why are you introducing the concept to the children in that way? Why are you going to have them work in pairs and not independently or in small groups? Why are you starting the lesson with the children sitting on the rug? Why did you choose these materials? Why this minilesson approach? Why have you chosen these students to assist you? Why did you choose this activity to teach the content objective? These questions are just a taste of the extensive list we discussed one afternoon over a cup of coffee.

After we mulled over these lesson questions, our focus turned toward how the lesson was to be managed. In this case, Scott and I had developed a collective understanding about the sort of management expectations Scott had for the children. Now, the key was to grapple with *how* to make it happen in the classroom context. How will you give the directions to the class? How will you direct the students back to their seats? How will you get their attention when their minds start to wander? How will you call them down to the rug? By group? By readiness? Individually? How will you communicate your behavioral expectations to the students? How will you signal to them that their work time is coming to an end? How will you be able to tell from their engagement that they are ready to continue with the lesson's activities? This lengthy collaborative process was indeed draining, yet at the same time exhilarating for both Scott and me. Upon leaving that bagel shop I could feel that Scott was about to teach a lesson vastly different from the previous one.

It is with a broad smile that I can say that my prediction became undeniably a reality. Was the lesson perfect? No way! That doesn't exist, remember? But it was fantastic. Always one to succeed in other arenas by going with the *flow*, teaching presented Scott with a fierce challenge. No longer able to "wing it" (his words), Scott visually grasped through this lesson enactment the entwined connections between comprehensive, deliberate planning and classroom management. Scott, by his own admission, felt disheveled and disorganized when he began his student teaching placements and was responsible for planning and teaching a whole class of children. Over the course of his final 2 months of student teaching, Scott began to see how classroom management could not be divorced from planning, and learned that teaching was not something that you could just "wing"; he must, through concise planning, create his own *flow*. Scott essentially demanded that I, not only explicitly say, "Hey, these are all the items you need to consider . . . ," but sit and work through the entire planning process (from start to finish) collaboratively with him.

The Instruction Lens—Leslie

Like the other student teachers, Leslie recognized that meaningful curriculum for the children cannot take place in any classroom until the trust between the teacher and students is established. With the relationship between Leslie and her students strong, she turned toward learning to create curricular events in which all children were both supported and challenged. Probably every novice enters the profession teaching with a vision of the "ideal" lesson. Within weeks of beginning their educational preparation coursework, student teachers can rattle off words to describe this perfect teaching event. To name a few: hands-on, cooperative, engaging, inquiry-based, and student-centered. As those of us who have been teaching for a while understand, creating dynamic educative events of this sort is complicated, sophisticated, and taxing. Likewise, even when the planning has been so deliberately thought out, and the execution played over and over in our minds, what actually unfolds may not turn out exactly as we have visualized. While experienced teachers may be fully cognizant that an alternative outcome may in fact be a good thing or at least an educative development, for many beginning teachers this can be devastating.

Grounding Leslie's every decision was the belief that each child in her classroom was a full and vital member of the community. From this theoretical vantage point we dissected what it takes to develop and enact curriculum events that are accessible, meaningful, and engaging for each and every student right from the start. Due in part to our dual system educating most students classified as "regular" or "normal" separately from those labeled as "disabled," many novices bring with them the belief that most, if not all, of their children will master the same academic content and skills at the same time. Though other preservice teachers may not radically critique the concept of "normal" as these novices did, most student teachers quickly realize that the children in their classrooms are widely diverse in a number of ways. This realization presents student teachers with the challenge of moving beyond developing a single format lesson and toward thinking more broadly about curriculum, achievement, individuality, and accessibility. I worked alongside Leslie as she plotted her own course for learning; all the while supporting her in her own inquiries and asking several of my own pointed questions.

In my experience student teachers work incessantly to identify the "answers" or "secrets," if you will, to becoming an outstanding teacher. Likewise, they assume that if a supervisor asks a question, then surely there must be a "right" answer out there somewhere and all they have to do is locate it. Leslie was initially no different in this regard, but quickly came to understand that teaching was complicated and that at times pondering the questions and investigating all the innovative options, was far more rich and educative than arriving at simple answers. As a team we inquired, discussed, silently pondered, and passionately collaborated about instructional issues stemming from these types of questions. What makes a lesson meaningful and authentic for all children? Do all the children have to achieve or even work on the exact same objective in the exact same way to make the lesson a success? What does it look like, sound like, feel like when all the children are engaged in the curriculum enactment? Can we pinpoint moments within the lesson that were absolutely powerful? Why were these moments so amazing? Then what can we learn from those moments so that we can apply this understanding toward creating future accessible curriculum events? I worked tirelessly to get Leslie (and really all of the teachers) into a frame of mind where they could enter any classroom and inquire: "What can I learn from this event?" What worked? What didn't? And perhaps most critically, "WHY?"

It was out of these conversations that Leslie was able to hone her planning and teaching to create the dynamical and completely engaging math cooperative lesson she discussed in her chapter. The power of the cooperative math lesson was that it supported and challenged the full range of students in her classroom. By starting the lesson reading *Strega Nona* to the whole class, each student was able to construct personal and shared understandings of the text they could apply to the task of completing the assigned chores. Likewise, when designing the broad task in which an infinite number of choices could be made to achieve the final goal (i.e., completing all the chores), Leslie provided room for the students to become agents of their own learning. One particular challenge when designing curriculum experiences that are so rich with student choices is assessment. Thus, questions around the concept of evidence are so critical.

By letting go of the idea that all children had to do, say, achieve, and complete learning events in the same way and within the same period of time, Leslie widened her vision of achievement and instruction, which in turn allowed her to imagine endless curriculum possibilities for every child. Moreover, from this standpoint, Leslie was able to deliberately create places where the children could carve out their own space to plan, theorize, examine, and problematize both individually and cooperatively how they would reach the lesson's goals and objectives. She set the outcome, scaffolded their learning, and facilitated the process, and in the end, the learning experiences that were most accessible and meaningful were those in which the children had room to pave their own path: much the same way I supported and challenged Leslie's own growth.

MY OWN JOURNEY AS A SUPERVISOR

The questioning approach I took with these student teachers certainly was not exclusive to spurring their own reflection and practice, but also sparked my own. Probably the question I most frequently ask myself continues to be "What can I do and say to best facilitate and stimulate their growth as novice teachers?" It should come as no surprise then that Jennifer, Carine, Barbara, Scott, and Leslie were not the only teachers who plotted a course and embarked upon a learning journey. As a future teacher educator completing my doctoral work I traveled a course that in several ways paralleled the routes taken by these student teachers.

What drives my work is the hope that the novices with whom I collaborate walk away from our tenure together with the understanding that the nuances of creating curriculum that is accessible to all children is a complex endeavor in a shifting educational terrain. Thus, there are no "right answers" when to comes to teaching, but rather, thoughtful, deliberate educative practice demands a constant cycle of simultaneous reflection and action (Freire, 1970). As the year unfolded and this chapter now draws to a close, I realize that several of my passionately held beliefs about teaching, learning, inclusion, and accessible curriculum have not so much changed, as much as they have become more crisply viewed through my own supervisory lens.

As an experienced elementary teacher of inclusive classrooms I understand that children are neither blank slates nor clay to be molded. Children simply do not learn the same way, look at life, school, or a specific content objective similarly, and thus cannot take away from a learning event the exact same understandings. Clearly, these assertions can also be applied to the learning of adults, and in this particular case, student teachers. After all, as any classroom educator will tell you, learning to teach did not begin and end during their preservice teacher education program. Instead the multitude of life experiences teachers accrue prior to entering a teacher preparation program, in addition to those they have after becoming teachers powerfully shape the curriculum and learning environments they construct with their students (Bullough, Knowles, & Crow, 1992; Powell, 1992).

Learning-to-teach is thought by many educators to be a constructive, always evolving process in which individuals interpret and filter new teaching experiences and information through their own existing beliefs, personal knowledge, values, and personal biographies (Britzman, 1986; Clandinin, Davies, Hogan, & Kennard, 1993; Pajares, 1992; Powell, 1996). With this understanding closely within view, I have become more firmly rooted in the belief that learning to teach is not a linear process, but dynamic, fluid, and always connected to an individual's values and life experiences.

Reflecting upon the vast diversity of my experiences with these remarkable novices, I am struck again by the obvious connection between my educative relationship with them and that between the student teachers and their own young students. If, as teacher educators, we are trying to instill within our students the notion that a single format lesson doesn't work for a widely varying group of children, why would we think it could possibly be successful with student teachers? Our journey together has provided me with an unwavering conviction that a one-size-fits-all supervisory approach is potentially disastrous and surely ineffective when working with student teachers in their quest to become agents of change. Perhaps then, if we understand learning to be fluid, the most transformative approach any supervisor and teacher educator can take is to model an accessible, personalized teaching perspective with our preservice teachers in the hope that they too will come to embody this approach when teaching inclusively in their own classrooms.

QUESTIONS

For Discussion and Reflection

- As a student teacher what can you do to promote a positive, collaborative relationship with your cooperating teacher and supervisor?
- Think about a lesson you taught recently or are in the process of planning. Generate and answer several key questions to help you reflect on "why" you made or will make each action in the lesson.
- Think about how you manage the students in your classroom. How do your management decisions show your children you respect them as people?

In the Field

- List some of the ways your supervisor supports your growth. How might your supervisor challenge you to take additional risks in your student teaching placement? How might you capitalize on the expertise he or she brings to you?

- Teaching is incredibly hard work. Student teachers often feel overwhelmed by the work and begin to doubt their abilities at times. What are your strengths at this point? Which aspects of teaching would you like to improve? What steps can you take to grow as an educator?

Chapter 8

Being an Inclusive Teacher

Celia Oyler and Britt Hamre

> *It is difficult to swim against the tide. But this is our most difficult task if our position in history is not to preserve the past, but to change the present to create the future.*
>
> —Freire (1985, p. 13)

Early on in Scott's third year of teaching in Brooklyn, he called one of his first graders' homes to find out why the child had not come to school that day. Scott knew the parents were separated and that the boy spent weekends at the family house in Queens where he and his mother would meet up with his father. The mother delivered news that nothing had ever prepared Scott to deal with: The boy's father had committed suicide. "Would you come and see him?" the mother asked Scott.

Scott made his way to Queens, wondering what he might be walking into when he got to the family home. He barely knew the family—it was only the second week of school—and he had never had a child in his class whose parent had died; nor did Scott have any experience with families encountering suicide. The emotional context became even more complex when Scott suddenly realized that the mother was asking Scott to be the one to tell the son that his father was dead. Apparently, they had explained to the 6-year-old that his father was taken to the hospital and was very sick, but no one had known how to break this final, grim news. The family had decided to wait for the teacher who would know what to say. Although incredibly intimidated, Scott found the words he needed to explain to this young child that his father had died and was not coming back.

It is clear from this story that teaching is filled with ethical decisions, moral challenges, and emotionally laden pedagogical dilemmas. Indeed, as teachers, we must be prepared to face the unexpected on a daily basis. Yet, when most students first enter their teacher education programs, they often expect that they will be taught the "best methods" for teaching. They ask: What are the recommended instructional methods?; What classroom management strategies work?; What are the best curriculum materials?

MOVING BEYOND THE TECHNO-RATIONAL

However, these questions that often spring most readily into the hearts and minds of preservice teachers must be seen as "technicist" or "techno-rational" concerns. From a techno-rational perspective teaching is seen as a series of steps that can be mastered; or as a set of competencies that can be taught, measured, and then add up to effective teaching. And, indeed, there are many "technologies" of teaching (Hinchman & Oyler, 2000), such as knowing various specific strategies for teaching reading, or having a set of questions one asks oneself while selecting children's literature, or having a clear plan for organizing materials distribution in the classroom. Yet, there is danger in thinking that if you know enough such technologies, then you will know how to teach. Rather, it is in the judicious employment of these technologies where teachers' daily decisions lie.

In the student teachers' inquiries presented in this book, we can see that questions about what to do in specific situations were often at the heart of their initial inquiries. Yet the answers that these beginning teachers arrived at made their more technicist questions fade; what supplanted their early "what to do next" questions were more complex investigations of the role of relationships and context in making all teaching decisions. In examining each of these student teachers' inquiries, we can trace this journey from technical to relational knowing; from propositional knowledge questions being at the base of their inquiries, to situated knowledge being offered as first answers.

CREATING AN ACCEPTING LEARNING COMMUNITY

Carine Allaf's inquiries led her to investigate the effects of two different service delivery models on the outcomes for students in inclusive classrooms. Yet, as you read her chapter and follow the day-to-day stories of life in the fifth-grade classroom with the part-time consulting teacher as compared to the first-grade full-time coteaching team, you notice that the narratives all center on the ways that people are or are not integrated into the learning community of the classroom. In the classroom where individual difference is sometimes scorned and derided, it is painful to read that not only are the students with disabilities targeted, but all learners are put on notice that they, too, may be next. In one vignette, the teacher singles out Anna for her exemplary work on her timeline that all students had been assigned for homework.

This example of Anna is a rich one to explore. Teachers *do* need to recognize exemplary work and help all students accomplish their very best. Since most of us who become teachers have been schooled in an environment based on competition, it is easy to see how Carine's cooperating teacher could have thought that praising Anna's work in specific and sustained ways would help motivate the other students to do similar work in the future. However, this action can be understood as problematic for a few different reasons. First, as Carine pointed out, children have different material resources at home, thus such projects and subsequent teacher approval and praise work to reinforce status differentials, rather than work to equalize them (Cohen & Lohtan, 1997). Second, when success is located in one individual, the rest of the class members are constructed as losers. Of course supporters of competitive motivational strategies believe that students have to learn that there are winners and losers in our capitalist society. However, this way of looking at student motivation is lacking in nuance. Rather than a zero-sum game, encouragement—rather than praise—(Dreikurs, 1964) can be offered to all students, contingent upon their need. This notion of contingent responsiveness (Wells & Chang-Wells, 1992) requires teachers to engage in close student observation and assessment. In this way, all students are held accountable to specific learning standards, but these standards are not generic, inflexible, or linear. From this perspective, it is not the teacher's job to find all the mistakes the student has made, but to find their *approximations.* This view holds that "children are always modifying the ideas and concepts in their schemas. Their present theories are tentative and approximate adult (or expert) views regarding a topic. . . . Approximations are the natural result of learning. . . . They reflect the linguistic and cultural diversity that children bring to their communication and approaches to learning" (Pappas, Keifer, & Levstik, 1990, p. 38). It is the teacher's job then, to work as a detective: becoming proficient at recognizing and acknowledging each student's approximations and helping scaffold them to the next step.

INVESTIGATING OUR ASSUMPTIONS
ABOUT CHILDREN

Working to understand individual children's approaches to learning is the basis for the assignment of a "child study" (Goodwin, 2002) or a "descriptive review of a child" (Himley, 2000) found in many teacher education programs (Cochran-Smith, 2004). This type of assignment helps student teachers to ask questions about learners based on work samples and close observations (Almy & Genishi, 1979). This is a view of teaching, not as an acquisition of generic "best practices," but rather a determination to look at each learner directly. As Leslie Gore explained in a recent conversation about her teaching, "This means that a teacher is not so much concerned with what a child *cannot* do, or what a child *is not* as with what a child *can* do, or who a child *is*—what he or she values, loves, is excited by, finds important, or essentially, what that child is really about."

This style of close observation and description requires teachers to first carefully interrogate their own assumptions while describing and analyzing the learner. Our own assumptions as teachers grow out of so many social and cultural factors. Thus our views of what a "good student" is and does are developed as young children in our first experiences negotiating between home and school. When there is a close match between school and home in terms of language, dialect, what is valued, discourse style, attitudes toward authority, beliefs about learning, and images of our place in society, there may be few opportunities to closely examine our own tacit assumptions.

Our assumptions act as filters through which we see all that takes place in our classrooms. This can be aptly demonstrated by carefully examining a data collection piece that a student teacher (whom I will call Nalisha) wrote for her child inquiry assignment. (This assignment is described in more detail in chapter 1.) Nalisha was using a three-part format recommended in *Ways of Studying Children* (Almy & Genishi, 1979, pp. 36–39) where she carefully described what she saw and heard, then noted her feelings about the observation, and then concluded with the inferences she made.

Child Study Piece #2

Description.   Amanda was sitting on the floor of the hallway with three other students and they were all learning to read the book *GO GO*. The teacher first read the book aloud, "Go cat, go dog, go duck, etc." All of the students were trying to read along following the teacher's "magic finger." Amanda sat cross-legged right in front of the teacher's legs. Her head was cocked all the way up to be able to see the book because she was sitting so close to the teacher. As the teacher was reading through the book, she started to read along with her, however instead of reading along she would actually repeat each word the teacher said one second after it was read aloud. The teacher then stopped, looked down at Amanda and said, "Sweetie, for now I just want you to pay attention to the way that I am reading it, you can read along with me in your head. I would like all the students to be able to hear me ok?" Amanda did not utter one word, but nodded her head up and down three times to acknowledge her teacher. The second time the teacher read through the book she asked all the children to read aloud with her. Amanda again repeated each word a fraction of a second after the teacher read it. The students were then split up into groups of two to read their books with a partner.

Amanda and her partner were sitting on the floor of the hallway against the sidewall near the staircase. There was a lot of noise coming from the other classrooms and the staircase, because teachers were teaching lessons, and students were running up and down the stairs while screaming things to one another. Amanda and her partner Sam opened their books together. Sam began saying, "Go cat" while Amanda said, "Look at the cat, he looks all funny." Sam said, "Yeah it does look real funny," as the two began to giggle. Amanda then turned the page and said, "I am gonna read this page. The duck was swimmin' in the lake and the sun was shining." She read this sentence using her finger to point to the words "go duck." She continued to go through the book and make up elaborate sentences instead of reading the two words written on the page. Sam just sat there silently and listened to her read her page, then when she finished he would read what was written correctly on the next page (as they were taking turns page to page).

Feelings.   The atmosphere that these children were working in to learn to read upset me. Children need a quiet space to read, especially when they are first beginning to read, as many of these children were. I was also very shocked at Amanda's reading level. As I stood there listening to her make up her sentences, I noticed that she basically looked at the pictures and made up elaborate sentences, but the teacher went through the book twice and clearly pointed out each word. I am wondering why her reading level is so low.

Inference.   Perhaps Amanda is classified as special education because she is a slow learner. I thought that in order to be in first grade children had to have some idea of print, but she seems to have minimal experience with reading. It is interesting how she followed along with the teacher the second time around and repeated each word perfectly, but just a few minutes later she had almost forgotten the pattern. I am wondering if all the books she used in Kindergarten were picture books. She has a very vivid imagination and articulates herself well. She can also recognize the correct animals throughout the book, but she does not have any pattern recognition or concept of a word. I am curious now to what her IEP states. I am wondering what Amanda will need in order to become a successful reader. I have now observed her in math and reading, and in both cases she seems to be a little behind the rest of the students.

Nalisha—the student teacher who collected this data piece and wrote the subsequent interpretation—does an excellent job of keeping her feeling and analysis separate from the description of what she actually observed. It is a valuable exercise for her to explore her feelings about the learning environment and the learner herself. Upon reading this assignment (and other students' similar write-ups) all the student teachers were asked to identify assumptions they were making and to explore the roots of these assumptions.

For Nalisha, although there was no evidence provided that the hallway noise was distracting to the children, she was surprised that this venue was being used to learn to read. She later related that in her own schooling experience, reading was a quiet affair that did not involve buddy reading or much talking among peers. Furthermore, and in common with many preservice students, Nalisha was not able to see the many approximations that Amanda did make in this literacy event. In fact, Amanda can be seen actively deriving meaning from text, cooperating with a peer to take turns and buddy read, using pictorial cues for comprehension, demonstrating various skills of print awareness, and using complex oral language.

However, Nalisha is looking not for Amanda's approximations, but instead for her compliance with the teacher's directions. She realizes from this observation that although Amanda has heard the teacher read the book out loud a number of times, she is not able to produce the few words actually printed on the page. This distresses Nalisha and she wonders how Amanda can be in first grade without knowing the words that are on the page. It is precisely at this critical juncture that Nalisha's expectations and assumptions about learning and learners must be challenged and deepened if she is to become a successful teacher of *all* students. Expecting that students will all be able to accomplish certain, specific tasks at a certain grade level is antithetical to an inquiry stance that asks teachers to look closely into each child's learning patterns.

Nalisha can also be seen here as having some strong expectations about normalcy and even abnormalcy. Confused by what she has observed with Amanda's buddy reading, and not having any specific knowledge or information that can help her understand the emergent literacy efforts of the student, Nalisha falls back on what she has learned somewhere in her past: Perhaps Amanda is a "slow learner." Clearly, this is not a label that comes from special education, or any of the coursework Nalisha has taken in her teacher education program. But it is a cultural concept in circulation for at least a century. (Think, for instance, of New York's public school classrooms started at the turn of the 20th century for "backwards youth"; Franklin, 1994.) Despite Nalisha's best efforts to understand the literacy progress of the student she was observing, her strategy of relying on prior assumptions from her own schooling experiences was not helpful in getting close to understanding the approximations of this young learner.

VIEWING DISABILITY DIFFERENTLY

Learning to look for students' approximations rather than errors is difficult work. It goes against some of our tendencies toward critique, tendencies that have been learned by attending school for 17 years before we become

teachers. As Barbara Wang points out in her chapter: "Consciously or unconsciously how, and in what environment, we were raised affects who we
are today. And as teachers, this translates into the way we teach and respond
to children." Throughout her chapter, Barbara keeps track of how she
thinks about and responds to children whose behaviors challenge the carefully laid plans of teachers. In three different settings, she notes how in every class there are students who are on the "outskirts" of classroom socialization and work.

> I constantly found myself distinguishing between "those" kids and "everyone"
> else. I don't know why. Perhaps it was because the teachers did. Maybe it was
> because the children did so as well. When I prioritized my time that's how the
> breakdown was—children with special needs and children without. And at
> the time, I did make that distinguishing factor, I did so without much thought
> or hesitation. I have to admit that I did many things early on without thinking.
> It wasn't until much later that I could recognize or even consider alternative
> reasons for my categorization.

Categorizing students into "regular" and "special" does not disappear with
the implementation of inclusive classrooms. In fact, by having a special education teacher designated to provide special education services mandated
through an Individual Educational Plan, the categories of "typical" and
"special" are, in fact, reified.[2]

But we also must be cognizant that our categories of "normal" and "ab-
normal" or "typical" and "atypical" or disabled or nondisabled are created,
rather than natural. Careful study of how our society has historically treated
people with mental illness, deafness, or intellectual disabilities, reveals that
our understanding of human variation or difference has changed over
time, and indeed is constructed differently across the world. One of the
most valuable contributions of disability studies scholars and disability
rights activists has been to document and describe the range of orientations
toward disability seen throughout the world.

The most common approach, and the one from which special education
is derived, views disability in a medicalized manner. From this position, a
disability is a pathology and a deficit. Responses to pathologizing disability
have ranged from the marginalization and segregation of those with disabilities, to a rehabilitation orientation, or a benevolence approach. Although
many historic examples of segregation and marginalization exist—such as
asylums and institutions—there are contemporary examples as well. For instance, living in the United States today, there are thousands of young and
middle-aged adults with significant physical disabilities who are ware-

---

[2]We should not be misunderstood here as arguing for the end of IEPs or protection of students with disabilities.

housed in nursing homes, even though all they need is in-home attendant care (Russell, 1998). This example is one that evidences our society's continual acceptance of the marginalization of people with disabilities. Self-contained special education classrooms still exist as a result of society's orientation toward segregating and marginalizing disability.

Also from the medical model, and along the same lines as marginalization, a rehabilitation orientation views disability as a personal deficit when compared to the "normal" population (Oliver, 1990, 1996; Van der Klift & Kunc, 1994). However, instead of entirely segregating or avoiding the disabled person, the goal of rehabilitation is to treat, reform, and assimilate the individual's defect so that the person is as close to normal as possible. The teaching of oralism to deaf people was among the first significant historical events illustrating the rehabilitation orientation in the 1800s. This labor intensive technique for learning oral communication replaced the previously dominant instruction of sign language in deaf schools and underscored the belief that if deaf individuals learned to speak orally they could assume a full and functioning position in the community (Winzer, 1997). Today the medical profession with their scientific research and newest technologies focus primarily on research and rehabilitation. An exorbitant amount of money is allotted to research in an effort to identify cures for paralysis, blindness, deafness, as well as a host of other diseases and impairments (Russell, 1998). A significantly less percentage of money is used to provide services to people that are living with these disabilities (Russell, 1998).

Early efforts to mainstream students with disabilities into the general education environment grow out of this rehabilitation orientation. As such, mainstreaming was considered a viable option for only "those students who were considered to be most like 'normal' [children]" (Lipsky & Gartner, 1997, p. 77). In some cases students with disabilities were allowed to enter the general education environment and interact with their nondisabled peers during times such as lunch, recess, music, art, and physical education classes (and perhaps an academic subject), but only after they had acquired the social, academic, and physical skill levels necessary to function independently. The rest of the time these students were relegated to a more restrictive and segregated setting.

Another special education practice focused on rehabilitation as the resource model. Instead of spending most of their time in a self-contained special education setting, students in this case spend the majority of their time in the general education classroom. The students labeled as disabled are pulled out to receive remedial instruction to help them climb to the "level" of their peers in just those particular subjects in which their skills are identified as deficient. The rest of the time they are assumed to be able to keep up with their nondisabled peers, thus not requiring the general education teachers to alter their curriculum or instructional techniques in any way.

Closely tied to, and growing directly from a rehabilitation response to disability, is the benevolence approach. From this perspective, an individual's disability should be minimized, perhaps masked, but at all times tolerated (Van der Klift & Kunc, 1994; Kunc, 2000). Treating disabled people with benevolence is closely related to the previous position of regarding them as clients to be rehabilitated. Again, both are predicated on the idea of disability as deficit. These orientations differ in that from the benevolence perspective, although the disability is a liability, it is to be accepted with compassion. (In contrast, the rehabilitation response does not ever really accept the disability for what it is, but rather is focused on going to great lengths to remediate the problem.) Treating disability in a benevolent manner underpins many of our social organizations for disabled people (e.g., the Special Olympics and the Jerry Lewis Telethon). What is often obscured, especially for nondisabled people, is the paternalization and patronization that serve as foundations for such well-meaning benevolence (Charlton, 1998; Linton, 1998; Oliver, 1996).

In Barbara Wang's vignette about Sophie—the little girl with Down syndrome—you can clearly see how the children and teachers had developed a paternalistic approach to their interactions with her. Such paternalism grows out of lowered expectations, which in turn stem from seeing students with disabilities from a deficit, rather than a competency or capacity perspective.

At the crux of the disability rights' criticism of the medical model (from which marginalization, rehabilitation, and benevolence emanate) is the unquestioned acceptance by the professional field (and society at large) that there is a certain, unbiased definition of what constitutes a normal person. In contrast to the medical model of disability, a valuing of human diversity approach views disability as one of many human characteristics based on mostly socially constructed notions of difference. From this perspective, normality is viewed as a suspect category that serves only to highlight the values of a society that inscribes one position as normal, and all others as deviant. Disability here is not denied (e.g., paralysis is real), but its complications stem mostly from socially constructed barriers and attitudes. The disability itself is neither good nor bad, "It just is" (Charlton, 1998, p. 167). Disability can give rise to particular subject positions that inform one's identity and perspective. Thus, disability is an aspect of a person's identity, not all-encompassing, but one part along with race, ethnicity, class, gender, socioeconomic status, religious beliefs, sexual orientation, and countless other ways people are both different from, and the same as one another.

Yet, because of our disability-segregated society, most people who become teachers have not had many close encounters or friendships with people with disabilities. This lack of contact and the marginalization of people with disabilities, usually results in a lack of critical awareness of both the lives of people with disabilities and the ways that such isolation produces an uncritical social consciousness. That is, most people who become teachers are unaware of their own able-bodied and able intellectual status in the world. Thus their conceptions of what is normal remain unproblematized.

A parallel example from racial identity development is relevant here. Professor Beverly Tatum, when teaching a course on racism, asked students to describe themselves in terms of their class and ethnic backgrounds. One student, "summed up her middle-class, White, European background by saying, 'I'm just normal' " (Tatum, 1994, p. 464). Although describing her ethnic, not her intellectual or physical positioning, the student not only assumed the existence of some "normal" subject position, but claimed it as well.

IDENTIFYING CAPACITIES IN ALL CHILDREN

Holding on to a capacity perspective and fiercely viewing all students as learners often requires educators to "teach against the grain" (Cochran-Smith, 2001) and to "challenge the inequities that are deeply embedded in systems of schooling and society" (p. 4). That is, while all around you, students are being labeled as "gifted and talented" or "emotionally disturbed" or "at risk" or "from a good home," you have to develop a counternarrative: a story that understands such categories as suspicious and almost always unhelpful. After all, how does knowing that someone has labeled a child as "at risk" actually help you know what how to hook her in as a learner? How does the label of "ADHD" help you to create a plan with her for when she has "a million fireflies in [her] head" (as one of Jen's students explained)?

The student teachers in this volume ask us to take a second look at what we mean by normal and to see the problems that it holds for teachers. Throughout the year of student teaching, we follow the stories of Carine, Barbara, Scott, Leslie, and Jen as they work to understand the specific needs of children who do not fit neatly into the category of "normal." So many of these student teachers' inquiries revolve around pedagogical dilemmas that surface as a result of students for whom the routine structures do not seem to work. What is most instructive from these stories is to ask the question that these student teachers repeatedly turn to: "What needs to change in the environment so that this child can be successful?" And "What can I learn from re-examining my assumptions about this child?"

In Scott's chapter we hear of his dawning realization that he must work to uncover the specific interests of each child; he sees this as a puzzle that requires a special code (or key) to solve. This metaphor, of course, challenges any notion of "normalcy" or of linear child development that proceeds in stages. Rather, this way of puzzling through learner motivation and profile demands careful and respectful looking and listening. Again, this is a capacity approach, which does not seek to itemize deficits, but looks to uncover potentiality.

While working to finish this book, we visited and interviewed each of these former student teachers. One night, long after the other teachers had left the building, Leslie reflected on what matters to her as an inclusive teacher. Before the custodian came to ask us to leave the building, she explained:

> You have to see the potential in each child. If you can't see it, you have to find it. There's enormous potential in every single child. You have to believe that a lot is possible. It sounds ideal, but it's really fundamental. You might not necessarily be able to put a finger on what those possibilities might be, but the fact that they exist, what they could be or might be. There is always something. Too many people in this education system today look at a child and say, "The child is this, the child is that." It's like a deficit, always looking at what they can't do. That's part of the reason why I always feel so uncomfortable in those IEP meetings where the whole support teams sits down because they're saving time and they just jump right in with the tests. I always say, "Well so and so has so many strengths." They always look at me like, "We're here to talk about what the kid can't do."

In this way of thinking, Leslie can be seen *assuming competence* (Kliewer, 1998; Kluth, Straut, & Biklen, 2003) about all the learners in her classroom. From this perspective, then, it is her responsibility as teacher to carefully inventory her own assumptions as wells as work overtime to find the specific capacities of each child.

Some labels that educators commonly used in the past are no longer in circulation; take for instance the term from the 1960s of *cultural deprivation*. This was a phrase used to explain achievement gaps between children (usually children of color) living in poverty and those whose homes most closely matched those of school. Now, if an educator were to use such a term, people would look at you askance. At some point in the future, the labels of today will also fade into the woodwork of history. But in the meantime, there is much work to be done confronting ableism in education. Although racism and sexism and to a lesser degree heterosexism are recognized as serious challenges to fairness, equity, and democracy in our classrooms, schools, and societies, ableism is often not even acknowledged.

> Applied to schooling and child development, ableist preferences become particularly apparent. From an ableist perspective, the devaluation of disability results in societal attitudes that uncritically assert that it is better for a child to

walk than to roll, speak than to sign, read print than read Braille, spell independently than use a spell-check, and hang out with nondisabled kids as opposed to other disabled kids, etc. In short, in the eyes of many educators and
society, it is preferable for disabled students to do things in the same manner
as nondisabled kids. (Hehir, 2002, p. 3)

Turning ableism on its ear and critiquing the pervasive notions of what
constitutes a normal student is absolutely necessary if teachers are to genu-
inely accept the full spectrum of diversity their children bring to the learning environment.

CREATING THE VISION, SUSTAINING
ITS GROWTH THROUGH SOCIAL ACTION

Examining one's own assumptions around disability and ability is central to
the work of being an inclusive classroom teacher, but it is still another matter to deliberately organize and take steps to work for school-wide systemic
education and social change. As difficult as it may be to find balance between the classroom and the wider community and world, we can see from
the chapters in this book that teachers are inextricably woven into the webs
of the school and the school system. It is not entirely possible to just close
your classroom door and do what you think is best. As Jen Lee points out in
her chapter, it is also essential to analyze school culture and school policies.
She wrote:

> The inclusion movement recognizes that there is no single way to teach stu-
> dents and that all students are diverse. However, many school practices seem to
> go against these beliefs. High-stakes testing, student/class organization, and
> school-wide curriculum are some of the ways I saw school practices go against
> the ideals of inclusion in trying to make students all learn in the same way.

As Jen's commentary makes clear, teachers must be responsive to educational mandates over which they sometimes have little or no control. Yet, responding to external accountability systems and mandated curricular
changes does not require that teachers only comply and submit. In other
words, teachers truly can be activists, advocates, and public intellectuals
who take it upon themselves to "worry [about] the world and to believe that
there is a symbiotic relationship between the private world of the thinker
and the public world he or she wishes to address" (Donatich, 2001, p. 1).
Teachers must not be technicists who merely implement the work that others have mandated, but can view the wider educational arena as their responsibility as well. This can take various forms. For Jen Lee, this has meant
that she is active in a New York City group called "PENNY": Progressive Edu-

cation in New York. She relates how it is sometimes difficult to balance all the competing demands:

> What's hard is just finding balance in my own life and the life of my school. Also making decisions about if I want to stay at school and help organize the book room, or do I want to go to the PENNY meeting tonight. Or do I want to go to a rally this weekend or should I stay and write some anecdotal records? So it's kind of a balance. Both inside school and outside school activities really help balance me so it's hard to decide. . . . I feel like a lot of time gets stretched because I still want to involve myself in professional things, not necessarily pertaining to my classroom, but just developing more skills as an educator or being more reflective about my practice. But still you need to keep up with your classroom paperwork and with everything else that's going on in the world; there's enough for you to do outside of your school.

Even though the daily demands on teachers are great, it certainly is not desirable to abdicate responsibility for educational outcomes to policymakers, politicians, and district administrators. "We have some considerable evidence that those who merge roles as successful teachers, supportive colleagues, and school leaders are among the most powerful change agents in urban classrooms, schools, and communities" (Oakes & Lipton, 2003, p. 441). However, the work of teachers who serve as activists for public, inclusive education should also not be undertaken as a solitary, individualistic practice. The image of the lone knight charging into battle and often sacrificing one's life does not hold up as a long-range plan for educational change. The lone wolf approach to systems change almost inevitably burns out teachers, or cause them to lose their positions before they even have tenure. It is also incredibly lonely to pursue what you are convinced is right in a context where everyone around you seems content with the status quo. So where does that leave the new teacher?

We take much inspiration from the true story of Rosa Parks. As most everyone in the United States knows, one day Rosa Parks (an African American woman living in the Jim Crow South) refused to give up her bus seat to a White man. The tale as it is told in many children's books is that Ms. Parks was tired and that her actions sparked the long, but very successful Montgomery Bus Boycott (Kohl, 1995). This version of the story portrays social change as the work of brave individuals who are accidents of history. The more complex and more accurate accounting of what actually took place in Montgomery, Alabama at the beginning of the U.S. Civil Rights Movement, is that Ms. Parks and her peers on the Montgomery Women's Council and the NAACP had been meeting and deliberating about how to challenge the segregation on the city buses.

Ms. Parks had been selected to attend special workshops at the Highlander Folk School in Tennessee (Horton, 1998) where people were being

trained in organizing nonviolent social change. As Myles Horton, the
founder of the school, tells it:

> When she returned to Montgomery and refused to move to the back of the
> bus, even though her action was not prearranged and she acted individually,
> Rosa Parks operated with the full knowledge that for at least two years black
> people in Montgomery had been trying to set up a test case on the segregated
> buses. She knew the consequences of her actions, she knew she would be ar-
> rested. But she didn't think she was breaking the law, because she didn't
> think the segregation law, which was unjust, should be there. With that knowl-
> edge, Rosa wasn't only acting as an individual, she was acting in a way that was
> consistent with the beliefs of the black organizations in Montgomery. . . . By
> refusing to move from her seat, this gentle woman set thousands marching
> and made it possible for the rest of us to stand tall. (Horton, 1998, p. 150)

Clearly, there is a relationship among personal courage, social vision,
and sustained organization. For inclusive classrooms to become the new
standard for educational equity and excellence, teachers must organize
with others who are like-minded to sustain their vision of what kind of
school and world we want to create. The personal courage needed to challenge the status quo cannot be underestimated, but as with Rosa Parks,
when we band together, we are guaranteed to be working collectively,
rather than individualistically. It is collective wisdom that will keep us true
to our vision, and demand accountability and equity. Such organized work
for school and curricular change requires exactly what the student teachers
in this book have described: a willingness to examine and reconsider assumptions about others; a commitment to ongoing reflection on teaching
and learning; a spirit of inquiry that pushes to return again and again to the
questions; and the energy to enter into this work in the company of others.

References

Almy, M., & Genishi, C. (1979). *Ways of studying children*. New York: Teachers College Press.

Anderson, G. L., & Herr, K. (1999). The new paradigm wars: Is there room for rigorous practitioner knowledge in schools and universities? *Educational Researcher, 28*(5), 12–22.

Britzman, D. (1992). *Practice makes practice: A critical study of learning to teach*. Albany, NY: State University of New York Press.

Bullough, R. V., Knowles, J., & Crow, N. (1992). *Emerging as a teacher*. New York: Routledge.

Butchart, R. E., & McEwan, B. (1998). *Classroom discipline in American schools: Problems and possibilities for democratic education*. Albany, NY: State University of New York Press.

Champion, T. B. (2003). *Understanding storytelling*. Mahwah, NJ: Lawrence Erlbaum Associates.

Charlton, J. I. (1998). *Nothing about us without us: Disability oppression and empowerment*. Berkeley: University of California Press.

Clandinin, D. J., Davies, A., Hogan, P., & Kennard, B. (Eds.). (1993). *Learning to teach, teaching to learn: Stories of collaboration in teacher education*. New York: Teachers College Press.

Cochran-Smith, M. (1990). Research on teaching and teacher research: The issues that divide. *Educational Researcher, 19*(2), 2–11.

Cochran-Smith, M. (1991). Reinventing student teaching. *Journal of Teacher Education, 42,* 104–118.

Cochran-Smith, M. (1995). Color blindness and basket making are not the answer: Confronting the dilemmas of race, culture, and language diversity in teacher education. *American Educational Research Journal, 32*(3), 493–522.

Cochran-Smith, M. (2001). Learning to teach against the (new) grain. *Journal of Teacher Education, 52*(1), 3–4.

Cochran-Smith, M. (2004). *Walking the road: Race, diversity, and social justice in teacher education*. New York: Teachers College Press.

Cochran-Smith, M., & Lytle, S. L. (Eds.). (1993). *Inside/outside: Teacher research and knowledge*. New York: Teachers College Press.

Cohen, E. G. (1994). *Designing groupwork* (2nd ed.). New York: Teachers College Press.

Cohen, E. G., & Lotan, R. A. (Eds.). (1997). *Working for equity in heterogeneous classrooms: Sociological theory in practice*. New York: Teachers College Press.

Darling-Hammond, L., French, J., & Garcia-Lopez, S. P. (Eds.). (2002). *Learning to teach for social justice.* New York: Teachers College Press.

Dewey, J. (1900). *The school and society,* and *The child and the curriculum: A centennial edition.* Chicago: The University of Chicago Press.

Dewey, J. (1916). *Democracy and education: An introduction to the philosophy of education.* New York: The Free Press.

Donatich, J. (2001). The future of the public intellectual. *The Nation* [Online]. Available: http://www.thenation.com/doc.mhtml%3Fi=20010212&s=forum

Dreikurs, R. (1964). *Children: The challenge.* New York: Duell, Sloan, & Pearce.

Duckworth, E. R., & the Experienced Teachers Group. (1997). *Teacher to teacher: Learning from each other.* New York: Teachers College Press.

Edwards, C. H. (2000). *Classroom discipline and management.* New York: Wiley.

Falvey, M., Givener, C., & Kimm, C. (1995). What is an inclusive school? In R. A. Villa & J. S. Thousand (Eds.), *Creating an inclusive school* (pp. 1–12). Alexandria, VA: Association for Supervision and Curriculum Development.

Fennimore, B. (1997). Moving the mountain: Assessment and advocacy for children. In A. L. Goodwin (Ed.), *Assessment for equity and inclusion: Embracing all our children* (pp. 241–259). New York: Routledge.

Fennimore, B. (2000). *Talk matters.* New York: Teachers College Press.

Franklin, B. M. (1994). *From "backwardness" to "at-risk": Childhood learning difficulties and contradictions of school reform.* Albany, NY: State University of New York Press.

Freire, P. (1970). *Pedagogy of the oppressed* (M. B. Ramos, Trans.). New York: The Seabury Press.

Freire, P. (1985). Towards a pedagogy of the question: Conversations with Paulo Freire. *Journal of Education, 167*(2), 7–21.

Ganser, T. (1996). The cooperating teacher role. *Teacher Educator, 31*(4), 283–291.

Giangreco, M. F., & Doyle, M. B. (2000). Curricular and instructional considerations for teaching students with disabilities in general education classrooms. In S. E. Wade (Ed.), *Inclusive education: A casebook and readings for prospective and practicing teachers* (pp. 51–70). Mahwah, NJ: Lawrence Erlbaum Associates.

Gitlin, A. (2000). The double-bind of teacher education. *Teaching Education, 11*(1), 25–30.

Goodwin, A. L. (2002). The case of one child: Making the shift from personal knowledge to professionally informed practice. *Teaching Education, 13*(2), 137–154.

Goswami, D., & Stillman, P. R. (1987). *Reclaiming the classroom: Teacher research as an agency for change.* Portsmouth, NH: Heinemann.

Hamre, B. (2003). *Getting it right from the start: Novice elementary teachers creating accessible curriculum for all students.* Unpublished doctoral dissertation, Teachers College, Columbia University.

Hamre-Nietupski, S., & Hendrickson, J. (1994). Regular educators' perceptions of facilitating friendships of students with moderate, severe, or profound disabilities with nondisabled peers. *Education and Training in Mental Retardation and Developmental Disabilities, 29,* 102–117.

Hehir, T. (2002). Eliminating ableism in education. *Harvard Educational Review, 72*(1), 1–32.

Himley, M., with Carini, P. (Eds.). (2000). *From another angle: Children's strengths and school standards.* New York: Teachers College Press.

Hinchman, K., & Oyler, C. (2000). Us and them: Finding irony in our teaching methods. *Journal of Curriculum Studies, 32*(4), 495–508.

Hollingsworth, S. (1994). *Teacher research and urban literacy education: Lessons and conversations in a feminist key.* New York: Teachers College Press.

Horton, M., with Kohl, J., & Kohl, H. (1998). *The long haul: An autobiography.* New York: Teachers College Press.

Hubbard, R. S., & Power, B. M. (1999). *Living the questions: A guide for teacher-researchers.* York, ME: Stenhouse.

Irvine, J. J. (2003). *Educating teachers for diversity: Seeing with a cultural eye.* New York: Teachers College Press.

Johnston, S. (1994). Conversations with student teachers: Enhancing the dialogue of learning to teach. *Teaching & Teacher Education, 10*(1), 71–82.

Kliewer, C. (1998). *Schooling children with Down syndrome: Toward an understanding of possibility.* New York: Teachers College Press.

Kluth, P., Straut, D., & Biklen, D. (Eds.). (2003). *Access to academics for ALL students.* Mahwah, NJ: Lawrence Erlbaum Associates.

Kohl, H. (1995). *Should we burn Babar?* New York: The New Press.

Kohl, H. (2001). New teachers and social justice. *NEA Today Online.* Retrieved January 3, 2003, from http://www.nea.org/neatoday/0103/intervw.html

Kohn, A. (1999). *Punished by rewards: The trouble with gold stars, incentive plans, A's, praise, and other bribes.* New York: Houghton Mifflin.

Kroll, L. R., LaBoskey, V. K., & Richert, A. (2002, April). *What makes a "good" student teaching placement? Lessons learned from a multi-year study.* Paper presented at the meeting of the American Educational Research Association, New Orleans.

Kunc, N. (2000, January 24). Handout. *Do All Kids Belong in All Classes?: Equity or Excellence in Public Education.* Retrieved July 2000 http://www.normemma .com

Ladson-Billings, G. (1994). *The dreamkeepers: Successful teachers of African American children.* San Francisco: Jossey-Bass.

Lave, J., & Wenger, E. (1991). *Legitimate peripheral participation.* Cambridge, England: Cambridge University Press.

Linton, S. (1998). *Claiming disability: Knowledge and identity.* New York: New York University Press.

Lipsky, D. K., & Gartner, A. (1997). *Inclusion and school reform: Transforming America's classrooms.* Baltimore: Paul H. Brookes.

McGregor, G., & Vogelsberg, R. T. (1998). *Inclusive schooling practices: Pedagogical and research foundations.* Baltimore: Paul H. Brookes.

Oakes, J., & Lipton, M. (2003). *Teaching to change the world* (2nd ed.). Boston: McGraw-Hill.

Oliver, M. (1990). *The politics of disablement.* New York: St. Martin's Press.

Oliver, M. (1996). *Understanding disability: Theory to practice.* New York: St. Martin's Press.

Oyler, C. (2001, Spring). Democratic classrooms and accessible instruction. *Democracy and Education, 14*(1), 28–31.

Pajares, M. (1992). Teachers' beliefs and educational research: Cleaning up a messy construct. *Review of Educational Research, 62*(3), 307–332.

Pappas, C. C., Keifer, B. Z., & Levstik, L. S. (1990). *An integrated language perspective in the elementary school: Theory into action.* White Plains, NY: Longman.

Pappas, C., & Zecker, L. B. (Eds.). (2001a). *Teacher inquiries in literacy teaching-learning.* Mahwah, NJ: Lawrence Erlbaum Associates.

Pappas, C., & Zecker, L. B. (Eds.). (2001b). *Transforming literacy curriculum genres: Working with teacher researchers in urban classrooms.* Mahwah, NJ: Lawrence Erlbaum Associates.

Peterson, M., Beloin, K., & Gibson, R. (1998). *Whole schooling: Education for a democratic society.* Detroit, MI: Renaissance Press. Retrieved November 6, 2002, from http://www .wholeschooling.net/

Peterson, M., & Hittie, M. (2003). *Inclusive teaching: Creating effective schools for all learners.* Boston: Allyn & Bacon.

Peterson, M., Hittie, M., & Tamor, L. (2002). *Authentic multilevel teaching.* Detroit, MI: The Whole Schooling Consortium. Retrieved November 6, 2002, from http:// www.wholeschooling.net/

Peterson, M., Tamor, L., Feen, H., & Silagy, M. (2002). *Learning together well: Lesson about connecting inclusive education to whole school improvement.* Detroit, MI: Whole Schooling Consor-

tium, Wayne State University. Retrieved November 6, 2002, from http://www.coe
.wayne.edu/CommunityBuilding/WSR%20AToc.html

Poetter, T. S. (1997). *Voices of inquiry in teacher education*. Mahwah, NJ: Lawrence Erlbaum Associates.

Powell, R. R. (1992). The influence of prior experience on pedagogical constructs of traditional and nontraditional preservice teachers. *Teaching and Teacher Education, 8*(3), 225–238.

Powell, R. R. (1996). Epistemological antecedents to culturally relevant and constructivist classroom curricula: A longitudinal study of teachers' contrasting world views. *Teaching and Teacher Education, 12*(4), 365–384.

Rilke, R. M. (1994). *Letters to a young poet* (M. D. H. Norton, Trans.). New York: Norton.

Rodriquez, A. (1998). Strategies for counterresistance: Toward sociotransformative constructivism and learning to teach science for diversity and understanding. *Journal of Research in Science Teaching, 35*, 589–622.

Russell, M. (1998). *Beyond ramps: Disability at the end of the social contract*. Monroe, ME: Common Courage Press.

Rust, F., & Koerner, M. (2002, April). *What makes a good student teaching placement: Overview of four years of study of multiple sites*. Paper presented at the meeting of the American Educational Research Association, New Orleans.

Salisbury, C., & Palombaro, M. (1998). Friends and acquaintances: Evolving relationships in an inclusive elementary school. In L. H. Meyer, H.-S. Park, M. Grenot-Scheyer, I. S. Schwartz, & B. Harry (Eds.), *Making friends: The influences of culture and development* (pp. 81–104). Baltimore: Paul H. Brookes.

Sapon-Shevin, M. (1999). *Because we can change the world: A practical guide to building cooperative, inclusive classroom communities*. Boston: Allyn & Bacon.

Schaffner, C. B., & Buswell, B. E. (1996). Ten critical elements for creating inclusive and effective school communities. In S. Stainback & W. Stainback (Eds.), *Inclusion: A guide for educators* (pp. 29–66). Baltimore: Paul H. Brookes.

Schon, D. (1983). *The reflective practitioner*. New York: Basic Books.

Schon, D. (1987). *Educating the reflective practitioner*. New York: Jossey-Bass.

Shapiro, E. S., Miller, D. N., Sawka, K., Gardill, M. C., & Handler, M. W. (1999). Facilitating the inclusion of students with EBD into general education classrooms. *Journal of Emotional and Behavioral Disorders, 7*(2), 83–93.

Skrtic, T. M. (1991). The special education paradox: Equity as the way to excellence. *Harvard Educational Review, 61*(2), 148–185.

Smith, T. E. C., Polloway, E. A., Patton, J. R., & Dowdy, C. A. (2001). *Teaching students with special needs in inclusive settings* (3rd ed.). Boston: Allyn & Bacon.

Snell, M. E., & Janney, R. E. (2000). *Practices for inclusive schools: Social relationships and peer support*. Baltimore: Paul H. Brookes.

Stainback, W., & Stainback, S. (Eds.). (1996). *Controversial issues confronting special education: Divergent perspectives*. London: Allyn & Bacon.

Stanovich, P. J. (1996). Collaboration: The key to successful instruction in today's schools. *Exceptional Children, 32*(1), 39–42.

Takaki, R. (1993). *In a different mirror: A history of multicultural America*. Boston: Little, Brown.

Tatum, B. D. (1994). Teaching white students about racism: The search for white allies and the restoration of hope. *Teachers College Record, 95*(4), 462–476.

Taylor, D. (1991). *Learning denied*. Portsmouth, NH: Heinemann.

Teel, K., & DeBruin-Parecki, A. (2001). *Making school count: Promoting urban student motivation and success*. New York: Routledge.

Thousand, J., & Villa, R. (1995). Managing complex change toward inclusive schooling. In R. A. Villa & J. S. Thousand (Eds.), *Creating an inclusive school* (pp. 51–80). Alexandria, VA: Association for Supervision and Curriculum Development.

Tomlinson, C. A. (1997). *Differentiated instruction: Facilitators guide.* Alexandria, VA: Association for Supervision and Curriculum Development.

Tomlinson, C. A. (1999). *The differentiated classroom: Responding to the needs of all learners.* Alexandria, VA: Association for Supervision and Curriculum Development.

Tomlinson, C. A., Callahan, C. M., Eiss, N., Imbeau, M., & Landrum, M. (1997). Becoming architects of communities of learning: Addressing academic diversity in contemporary classrooms. *Exceptional Children, 63,* 269–282.

Van der Klift, E., & Kunc, N. (1994). Beyond benevolence. In J. S. Thousand, R. A. Villa, & A. I. Nevins (Eds.), *Creativity and collaborative learning: A practical guide to empowering students and teachers* (pp. 391–401). Baltimore: Paul H. Brookes.

Villa, R., & Thousand, J. (1995). The rationale for creating inclusive schools. In R. A. Villa & J. S. Thousand (Eds.), *Creating an inclusive school* (pp. 28–44). Alexandria, VA: Association for Supervision and Curriculum Development.

Villa, R. A., & Thousand, J. S. (2000). *Restructuring for caring and effective education: Piecing the puzzle together.* Baltimore: Paul H. Brookes.

Watts, D. (1987). Student teaching. In M. Haberman & J. M. Backus (Eds.), *Advances in teacher education* (Vol. 3, pp. 151–167). Norwood, NJ: Ablex.

Wells, G. (Ed.). (2001). *Action, talk, and text: Learning and teaching through inquiry.* New York: Teachers College Press.

Wells, G., & Chang-Wells, G. L. (1992). *Constructing knowledge together: Classrooms as centers of inquiry and literacy.* Portsmouth, NH: Heinemann.

Winzer, M. A. (1997). Disability and society before the eighteenth century: Dread and despair. In L. Davis (Ed.), *The disability studies reader* (pp. 75–109). New York: Routledge.

Wong, E. D. (1995). Challenges confronting the researcher/teacher: Conflicts of purpose and conduct. *Educational Researcher, 24*(3), 22–28.

Zumwalt, K. (1988). Are we improving or undermining teaching? In L. Tanner (Ed.), *Critical issues in curriculum: Eighty-seventh yearbook of the National Society for the Study of Education* (pp. 148–174). Chicago: University of Chicago Press.

About the Authors

Carine Allaf was born in Lebanon on July 31, 1979. She lived in Kuwait until the age of 11. Carine and her family, completely unaware of what was happening in Kuwait, left less than an hour before Iraqi troops entered the country, for a summer vacation in the United States. Carine, her parents (Wafica and Ezzedine), sister (Nadine), and two brothers (Mohammad and Rabih) have been here ever since.

After attending middle and high school in the suburbs of Philadelphia, Carine attended Lehigh University where she played lacrosse and majored in psychology. She took many education classes and realized that she wanted to pursue her Masters in elementary education. She attended Teachers College, Columbia University, immediately after graduating from Lehigh.

Carine has returned to Lebanon where she is teaching second grade at an international school. In her free time, Carine likes to run, go to the gym, or read (especially children's books).

Leslie Gore, born of West Indian parents from Martinique and Antigua, grew up in Staten Island, New York with her parents and older brother. She, appreciating the vivacity and eclectic nature of urban life, often wondered why her parents settled in their working, middle-class neighborhood in one of the most suburban boroughs of New York City.

Although Leslie attended schools on the island, she pursued many extra-curricular interests, such as music and dance in Manhattan and Brooklyn. Comfortable with the life she had built and the vast intellectual and professional opportunities the city had to offer, she attended Columbia College,

Columbia University in New York City where she majored in history and in dance. Leslie graduated with a Bachelor of Arts degree.

After turning down acceptances to law school Leslie spent two years working with children, pondering her purpose in life, and reconsidering her long-lost goals and values concerning children, education, and social justice. Leslie made a decision to pursue an M.A. in Elementary Education at Teachers College, Columbia University.

Leslie graduated in May 2002 and now teaches fifth and sixth grade in a small, alternative, public school in East Harlem.

At the age of eight, **Britt Hamre**, the eldest of a lower middle-class Scandinavian family was intent on becoming a special education teacher. Like most children, career choices change over time, but after graduating from a performing arts public high school in Miami, Britt came to the conclusion that "struggling, starving actress" was certainly not the career title for her. Britt quickly refocused on teaching.

Always uneasy and incredulous of segregated education programs for students labeled as disabled, Britt found at the University of Wisconsin–Madison a special education teacher preparation program that aligned with her values of community, justice, equity, and inclusion. Adding to her special education degree, she attended Mercer University to pursue an M.A. in Early Childhood Education while teaching in Conyers, Georgia. There she held both special and general education inclusive teaching positions for 6 years.

Britt completed her doctoral degree at Teachers College, Columbia University and wrote her dissertation (*Getting it Right From the Start: Novice Elementary Teachers Creating Accessible Curriculum for all Students*) about three teachers from another year's Preservice Inclusion Group.

Scott Andrew Howard, an extremely proud member of a very large family, was born in Rochester, New York and grew up in a beautiful suburb of the same city, Fairport. Scott's German, French-Canadian, Irish, and midwestern (Wisconsin, Illinois, and Indiana) ancestors contributed to the production of his current family consisting of two sisters, Amy and Jenny, their families, the Greens and Albrechts, and a supportive, caring, and loving set of unique, and exceptional parents, Judy and Andy. All of Scott's family members including his six nieces and nephew (Autumn, Cory, Aaron, John, Megan, and Rachel) currently live outside of Rochester so going home to visit really means he's going home to the people he loves and adores (including a special group of friends with whom he still keeps in touch).

Scott graduated from the University of Michigan's School of Education where he majored in English and minored in Sociology. In addition, Scott received a secondary certification to teach both English and Sociology. Deciding to continue his study of education after college, Scott applied to Teachers College's Preservice Childhood/Elementary Education Masters Program. Although Scott grew up in New York State, he found himself in New York City for only the second time in the fall of 2000. After completing his Masters Program at Columbia University in May 2002, Scott began teaching first grade at a public magnet school for the arts in Brooklyn, New York. Scott continues to be inspired by everyone he meets.

After studying religion and public policy (focusing on educational policy) at Swarthmore College, **Jennifer Lee** joined Teach for America and taught elementary school in New Orleans for 2 years. She worked as the assistant program director for a literacy-based Americorps program in New Jersey before coming to Teachers College and joining the Inclusion Study Group. Jen is a consulting teacher at a progressive elementary school in Manhattan. In her spare time, she gets involved in different social justice events, visits her family and friends, watches movies, and tries her hand in crafts. She longs for her bike and traveling, and particularly to revisit New Orleans. Jen wants to thank Edwin and the members of the Inclusion Study Group for their patience and support throughout the writing process.

Celia Oyler is an associate professor in the Department of Curriculum and Teaching at Teachers College, Columbia University. She is the author *of Making Room for Students: Sharing Teacher Authority in Room 104* (Teachers College Press, 1996). Before completing her PhD in curriculum theory (University of Illinois, Chicago) Celia taught in public and alternative schools for 15 years in Connecticut, Vermont, and Chicago. Her work focuses on issues of social action, accessible curriculum development, and preservice teachers' ideas on diversity and social justice.

Barbara Wang, a Midwestern girl at heart, was born in Michigan and raised in Madison, Ohio. There, her family (father, Peter, mother, Deniece, older sister, Angela, and two cats) maintained a working, middle-class lifestyle in small town suburbia. After graduating from Madison High School, Barbara went on to study at Washington University in St. Louis where she majored in psychology and minored in fine arts. Upon completing her bachelor's degree, she moved back home to Madison for 2 years, where her adventures back into the "educational compound" first began. The dichotomous struggle arising from her hyphenated ancestry (she is Chinese-American), led her to seek solace in the diversity of New York City, where she completed the Preservice Childhood/Elementary Education Masters Program at Teachers College, Columbia University in May 2002. Barbara is a kindergarten teacher in Manhattan.

Author Index

Subject Index